Dancing in Rhythm with the Universe

10 Steps to Choreographing Your Best Life

Learn how to step out of chaos and step into your outrageous self!

Barbara Miller

OTHER BOOKS WRITTEN BY BARBARA

Keto for Life, 28 Day Fat-Fueled Approach to Weight Loss

How to Write a Book and Tell Your Story, Easy Steps to Write, Publish and Promote Your Book

You Lost Your Marriage Not Your Life, How to Create the Life You Want Your way

You Lost Your Marriage Not Your Life, Positive Thoughts Journal

Disclaimer

The intention of this book is to provide information and encouragement to the reader. It is not intended to counsel or give medical advice in any way. The material in this book is the author's opinion only.

The author is not a doctor and does not treat or diagnose any medical conditions. The information in this book is not intended to replace any advice given by your doctor. There are many other resources available on information contained in this book. The reader is advised to do their own research on topics mentioned in this book.

Barbara & Company International, Inc. Trade Paperback Edition

New revised version 2022

Published in the United States by Barbara & Company International, Inc.

ATTENTION CORPORATIONS, UNIVERSITIES, COLLEGES, and PROFESSIONAL ORGANIZATIONS: Quantity discounts are available on bulk purchases of this book for educational or gift purposes, or as premiums for increasing magazine subscriptions or renewals.
Special books or book excerpts can also be created to fit specific needs.

Printed in the United States of America www.barbaraandcompany.com

DEDICATION

This book is dedicated to my wonderful husband and friend David. You have supported my project and encouraged me every *word* of the way. Thank you from the bottom of my heart.

CHAPTERS

"There are three words that convey the secret of the art of living, the secret of all success and happiness: One with Life. Being one with life is being one with Now. You then realize that you don't live your life, but life lives you. Life is the dancer and you are the dance."

Eckhart Tolle, A New Earth: Awakening to Your Life's Purpose.

Imagine the entire universe dancing and spinning all around you complete with beautiful lights and sounds. You are directing a special symphony to an expanding orchestra and are choreographing your own dance. Life will manifest your dance exactly as you instruct it. It's your turn! Shall we dance?

ACKNOWLEDGEMENTS

It is with a full heart that I say "thank you" to the beautiful women you will read about on the pages of this book. I have been blessed beyond measure because of you and your willingness to share your lives with me. You are the real message I speak of and my prayer is that you have also been blessed and encouraged on your journey called "life."

This book was written for you, the reader, that you might find insights and nuggets of wisdom to assist you in the daily art of living—one moment—one day at a time. I have gained so much from you and the personal experiences you have so graciously shared with me. You are the dance of these pages and may I always find you *Dancing in Rhythm with the Universe.*

Chapter 1
DANCE OF COURAGE

"Whatever course you decide upon, there is always someone to tell you that you are wrong. There are always difficulties arising which tempt you to believe that your critics are right. To map out a course of action and follow it to an end requires...courage."

Ralph Waldo Emerson

When I first moved to Naples, Florida, I was alone with little money and no job! I had just gone through a painful divorce and was now on my own. Why did I do it and where did I find the inner strength to make such a drastic decision? Somehow, not moving to Florida felt more wrong than staying put. Once I had made my decision and shared it with a friend, she said, "Barbara, you are such a strong courageous woman. I could never make a move like that." However, I did not feel strong and I certainly did not feel courageous; I felt compelled to make a change. I could hear my mother's voice saying, "You can do that. You have wanted to move to Florida for a long time so just go ahead and do it."

How was I able to pack up my belongings and move so far from home? Was I scared? No, I was terrified! I did not for one moment think that my move would be a breeze. Starting a few days before my move, I began experiencing intense panic attacks. How could I leave my home of twenty-seven years and my precious daughter? Because, deep in my soul, I knew it was what I really wanted and needed to do, and I had an inner knowledge that this was the right decision. This belief gave me the strength and courage to dare to make a change.

It was a real challenge to figure out how I was going to survive financially once I made my move to Naples, so I decided to handle the move myself. I rented the largest U-Haul truck they made and whatever I intended to take with me had to fit in that truck. I had rented a two-bedroom apartment and a one stall garage. The extra per month for the garage was less than a storage unit. I hired an experienced driver to drive the truck with a car carrier attached so he could bring my car and I could fly down and meet him at the apartment. I also had to fly him back to Grand Rapids, Michigan. I then hired three men over the phone from a local halfway house in Naples to unload the truck. I thought it was a great plan.

First of all, the driver arrived in Naples right on schedule but the three men did not. I was on the phone, frantically calling the woman in charge to find out what happened to the men. She informed me that they were running a little late. She had told them my job would take about three to four hours. I stood there, not knowing whether to scream or cry. I told her as calmly as I could that it took two experienced men eight hours to load my truck and my new apartment was on the third floor. There was silence on the other end. Finally, she said, "Oh, just tell them I didn't understand how much time was involved."

I was almost panic stricken by the time they arrived and when they stepped out of the car, I knew it was going to be a really long day. The first one was extremely overweight and out of shape. The next one I saw looked like he belonged in the hospital he was so emaciated. He looked to be about retirement age and had a terrible cough. He was puffing a cigarette as he struggled out of the car. At least the third man looked more promising as he was tall and nicely built and appeared to be around forty. This was my crew! My driver left and took a cab to the airport. The men took one look at the truck and three flights of stairs and threatened to leave, insisting they had never been told there was no elevator.

I begged and pleaded with them to the point of tears, explaining that I was here alone and had no one to turn to. They agreed to start as long as I paid them more and allowed them to put half of my belongings in the garage. I thanked God all day for that garage! I had to stand on the balcony and instruct them in what they needed to bring up and, of course, it was all the heavy furniture. Not too long into the project, the larger man walked in carrying my two beautiful elephant lamps. He then dumped them on the floor where they banged into each other and broke. I gasped and looked at him as he fumbled to try and grab the lamps. He braced himself for a confrontation. I was mortified but I knew there would be nothing to gain by screaming at him. I said, "It's okay, don't worry about it. He mumbled, "Sorry, Barbara."

Two hours had now gone by and the oldest of the three had taken numerous cigarette breaks. Finally, the more in shape one of the three began to complain. "Barbara, I am doing all the heavy work for this back-breaking job. The other two are not physically fit for hard labor. I am getting really pissed off at both of them." I noticed they started fighting with each other and snapping insults. Finally, when all three were taking a break

3

together, I said, "Look guys, I know this is a killer job for all of you and I intend to pay each of you an additional amount if you will please stay and finish the job."

Along Came Phil

That approach worked for another hour until the heavyset man began to complain. "Please, Barbara, I can't go on any longer. My calves are cramping and I can hardly walk." I was so close to dropping into a weeping heap. Suddenly, out of nowhere came the man I had met when my truck driver was unloading my car. He had introduced himself as Phil and started carrying on about how dirty my car was and he was going to wash it. He also said he worked there at the apartment complex and pointed out the little car wash area. The truck driver just looked at me and shrugged as Phil quickly washed down my car and drove it into a parking spot. This is when the truck driver left for the airport.

Four hours later, Phil turned up again and said, "What's going on here, Miss Barbara? I wondered how the unloading was going." I said, "Well, not so good right now as all three of them say they are quitting and are not going to finish the job." I could not believe his reply. "If you want to hire me, Miss Barbara, I will act as foreman and whip them into shape. Why did you hire these guys in the first place?" I just shook my head and refused to discuss it but I hired Phil for twelve dollars an hour, and he was worth so much more.

Once Phil took over as the leader and began shouting orders, everything changed. They demanded to know who he was and why he was bossing them around. He said, "I work for Miss Barbara. Look as this helpless little woman. You can't just leave her here with a truck to unload. Let's get moving and get this job done. It is New Year's Eve!" They continued to grumble every step of the way while Phil pushed, prodded and downright ordered them to move it! Halleluiah, they finished at six o'clock on New Year's Eve! As they were leaving, I realized that I had a truck to return to U-Haul! Phil said, "Don't you worry now, Miss Barbara. I am going to drive that truck and you follow me in your car." I did not know Phil or anything about him but he drove my truck and waited for me while I took care of the paper work. I then drove him back to the apartment complex. I have never been more grateful for my *angel unaware* in my entire life.

Phil announced when he left that night that he was also a weight trainer and in great shape and was going to come back after New Year's Day to help me organize everything. I dragged myself upstairs to my new home, looked around then sat down and cried. There was barely enough room to walk and my girlfriend was picking me up in an hour to celebrate the new year. I thought, well this is it, the beginning of my first year of new life in Naples, Florida.

I had left no room for failure in my move to Florida. I could not go crawling back home to Grand Rapids, Michigan defeated, as I had no home to crawl back to. I remembered a story my friend Karol had told me years ago about a man who lived in a tree. I don't remember the details of why he took up residence in a tree but I knew for certain I did not want that to be me! Therefore, I had no alternative other than success. Besides, I was on a mission I called "finding Barbara."

Barbara Miller

First of all, I needed to define who I was, who I had become and who I wanted to be. I began to realize that I would never be free to love and trust others until I learned to love and trust myself. That sounds simple enough but when it encompasses a lifetime, it is a daunting task. I have always been a *people pleaser* and sometimes that's acceptable, but where should I draw the line? I am also non-confrontational and when you combine that with pleasing people, you compromise yourself both emotionally and spiritually. I feel extremely selfish if I hurt someone by saying no. Sometimes I even feel afraid that I will lose their friendship or love. It is incredibly difficult to rid yourself of the fear of rejection but trust me when I say it is not impossible!

You do not need anyone's approval to be a secure and well-defined woman; and neither do I. My sister Carol once told me that I needed to stop feeling responsible for everyone and everything that crossed my path. What prompted this reprimand was when she had driven down state from Drummond Island, Michigan, to Grand Rapids to help me with my estate sale. Carol shared how she barely escaped what could have been a terrible car accident. As she described the event in detail, my response was, "Oh, thank God nothing happened while you were on your way to help me. If anything would have happened to you, I could never forgive myself." She looked startled and said, "Oh, Barb, our life growing up had a bigger impact on you than I realized. You are not responsible for me, and you cannot control what happens to me." What was it that made me feel responsible for whether she had an accident or not?

6

Eva's Story

I married a man that I was not totally in love with but after being alone for several years, I just wanted a married life again. I liked being a couple, not a divorcee. I guess I knew down deep that I was settling but he was attentive and we had a lot of fun together.

He was always telling me about his past life and how his wife was addicted to old movies and they spent every evening sitting on the sofa watching movies. I shared with him that I did not care much for television and an occasional movie was okay. He informed me that he never watched regular television as he refused to listen to or watch commercials. I agreed as long as I got to watch the world news.

Not much time had gone by when he started arriving home every night with not one but three videos at a time. I tried to convince myself that it really did not matter, but it did matter because I felt trapped and became so frustrated and controlled. My anger and resentfulness brewed inside like a smoldering volcano until my blood pressure soared dangerously high and I began to suffer from chronic insomnia. I tried to excuse myself and say I had seen enough movies for a while and wanted to relax with a good book. Then he began to sulk and withdraw and insist that I didn't love him anymore. I was forced to sit right there beside him until I thought I could crawl out of my own skin!

My desires for myself were being grossly violated. He now was insisting on eating dinner in front of the television so he could start his videos earlier. I was allowing this scenario out of fear of confrontation until I thought I might lose my mind. I felt sucked dry by a needy selfish man who cared only about his own needs, which was me by his side day and night. He knew I hated watching videos every night yet he could not seem to resist this habit. I believe he was trying to recreate his previous life. I grew to hate the entrapment I felt and eventually I grew to hate him! I finally filed for divorce and now realize that there are worse things than being alone. It took me a long time to learn the word "no" but this horrible experience taught me a lesson in how to stand up and take charge and stop allowing others to manipulate me. I feel safer now in relationships and in control instead of being controlled.

If you see yourself in Eva's story and there is still hope for your marriage, I strongly suggest that you insist on counseling. Compromising your life on a daily basis will ultimately lead to ill health and unhappiness and, as in Eva's case, divorce. Ask yourself these questions:

- What am I getting from this relationship?
- Do I feel uplifted by this relationship?
- Is this relationship fulfilling?
- What am I sacrificing by staying in this relationship?
- Does this man treat me respectfully?
- Does he value my feelings and opinions?
- Are mt decisions respected and trusted?
- Do I feel valued as the most important person in his life?

If you struggle to find positive answers to these questions, maybe it is time to do some serious digging deep inside. Ask yourself: *Why am I setting myself up for heartbreak and what motivates me to keep choosing men who use and abuse me?* Control is a form of abuse because it causes you to be subservient and compromise yourself. If you find no answers and he is unwilling to change, then seek help and above all, get out of that relationship! By staying you are protecting him while he is abusing you. Yes, you may feel committed to this man; however, the man who claims to love and cherish you should never verbally or physically abuse you. I realize that getting out of a marriage with no security is not the same as walking away or quitting a job, but we are talking about your life! Find the courage to seek help immediately!

Perhaps you have been conditioned in your past life to believe that this is what you deserve. This was how your father treated your mother and she tolerated it, so why shouldn't you? Maybe you never had the attention you needed as a child and no one seemed to even notice that you were around. I believe this is one of the reasons behind my mother's decision to stay in a life of physical abuse. She told me she never felt wanted or loved as a child and that she came and went as she pleased and no one even asked where she had been. She felt invisible and lonely. Her parents were wonderful people but not openly affectionate and loving. Subconsciously she may have thought this was not the type of relationship she wanted with my father but at least she was being noticed.

Barbara Miller

Sandra's Story

While working as an executive assistant in a stock brokerage company, I became very attracted to the head of the company and was pleasantly surprised when he invited me out for dinner. He was a high rolling stock broker and financial planner and lived the high life. He had a private jet and a fabulous home on the Gulf of Mexico. I was totally in awe of his lavish lifestyle and the fact that he wanted to share this with me left me spellbound.

We started dating on a regular basis and were together for two years when he asked me to marry him. I was bursting with joy as he told me to plan our wedding and spare no cost. I could have whatever I wanted. It was absolutely magical as we flew off to Tahiti for our honeymoon. However, upon returning home, things began to change. We were having a discussion one night and I was disagreeing with him about how he had handled a situation with one of his children. We were not even arguing when he stood up and slugged me in the face. I had to be rushed to the hospital as he had broken my nose.

He cried all the way to the hospital and begged me to forgive him. When the doctor asked me what happened, I said, "My husband hit me." The doctor wanted to call the police and insisted I file a formal complaint. My husband begged me not to report him and promised me it would never happen again. He was so remorseful I just could not bring myself to call the police. However, this was to be one of many trips I would make to the hospital over the next year. I always made up some excuse as to what had happened, never daring to accuse him again.

My son was outraged over what I was going through and insisted I get out of this man's home immediately. My son did not live in the same town and had a family of his own so I starting lying to him and assuring him that things were better. However, my best friend saw me on a regular basis and announced that she could not bear to see me go through this abuse another day. I was always trying to camouflage my bruises.

My husband threatened to kill me if I dared to leave him. He said he would find me and kill me and make it look like an accident. He started appearing at home unexpectedly at various times of the day. He would actually leave and say he was going out of town and then watch the house all day to make certain I did not attempt to leave.

My friend had devised a plan to get me out of the house and take me to the Women's Shelter. I was never so frightened in my entire life but I knew I had to get out or continue to be battered on a regular basis. My girlfriend followed him to work one day and after making sure he went inside, called me to be ready for her to pick me up. This was the day that forever changed my life. I walked out of his palatial home with nothing and walked into the Shelter for Abused Women and Children.

Now everything I experienced during that year seems like a bad dream. I don't know how I stayed so long. If my best friend had not helped me escape, I may have never lived to tell this story. I am now working at rebuilding my life and am still in counseling. My counselor is helping me understand why I was attracted to an abusive man and is giving me steps to take to build my self-esteem so I never make the same mistake again.

Women have been conditioned to ignore or deny their individual needs because we were programmed to meet the needs of our children and our husbands. We are expected to work in our home, church, school, various charities and volunteer for this and that until we are burned out and spent with nothing left for ourselves. Why? Because we want to please people, and most of all, we do not want to feel guilty! "No" brings guilt in a little two letter word and "no" brings fear of not being liked. We feel diminished for not meeting other's expectations of us.

Expectations

I shared in my book, *You Lost Your Marriage Not Your Life*, of how I lived in fear as a child that if I failed to behave as expected, I might be "sent away." This fear instilled in me the need to please and hide my true feelings so no one would be angry with me. This led to men who sensed my vulnerability. I was easily controlled and manipulated, which ultimately left me angry and depleted. When we have no control over our life, we can become stressed out, overworked and dried up emotionally. It reminds me of a story my sister Deb shared with me. Deb was babysitting a mouse for a friend. Yes, I said a mouse. This mouse liked to run on a tiny mouse treadmill. I was shocked to see this sport and found it quite amusing. It wasn't so funny when Deb called one morning to tell me she had killed her friend's mouse by overtaxing it on the treadmill. It literally ran itself to death! We do not want to be like that mouse and push ourselves over the limit.

You do not need to run your life on a treadmill to be validated. Allowing others to overtax and violate you until you are bone dry does not make for a happy fulfilling life. It is empty and confusing and will suck the life out of you! Remember our mantra from *You Lost Your Marriage Not Your Life*: *I am beautiful, I am strong, and I am a princess.* Stand up, princesses of the universe, and say NO!

Vicky's Story

I had always been an independent person and when I married Stan, I had no idea that he was going to be constantly checking up on me and violating my privacy in ways I had never experienced. I had always earned my own money and bought whatever I wanted with no one questioning me about how much it cost. I did not have any problem being accountable for large purchases, but one day I walked in and surprised him while on the computer combing through my personal checkbook entries. When I asked him what he was doing, he said, "I like to know where all the money goes and exactly what you are spending it on." I actually made more money than him and I was so offended I wanted to smack him. He had insisted that I let him set up all of my accounts online and use Quicken for my checkbook register. Now I knew why.

The next shock came when he appeared in the doorway holding my credit card statement. He demanded to know what a certain charge was for as it seemed rather high to him. I was livid! I told him it was for my new coat and he knew about that purchase. His response was, "I was just making sure that all of these charges are correct." With that I snatched the statement from his hand and said, "Please do not ever do that again, I am perfectly capable of checking my own statements." I know these were issues that should have been discussed before the marriage, but I never dreamed how far he would go until I caught him scrolling through my cell phone address book. When I asked him what the heck he was doing, he said, "Oh, I was just curious who you talked to on your cell phone because I noticed your cell phone bill is very high."

His need to know every detail of my life became so unnerving that I felt like I was living with a stalker. He actually started searching through my dresser drawers. When I caught him, he made some flimsy excuse that he was looking for an address he had on a piece of paper and thought maybe it was in one of the drawers. Yeah, right!

After two years, I could not take it anymore and filed for divorce. I was in a marriage with a severely paranoid man and I can say with all honesty, I did not do anything wrong to provoke this irrational behavior.

Had Vicky decided to stay in the marriage without addressing the issues with her husband, she may have felt trapped in a no-win situation which can lead to depression and inner anxiety. Living in an atmosphere of mistrust and privacy violation sets the stage for passive aggressive tactics that undermine the integrity of the marriage. I really do not know if Vicky could have avoided finding herself living in this situation. Probably the warning signs were there before the marriage and

Vicky chose to ignore them. It is possible that her husband worked at keeping his excessive need to see everything she was doing in check until after the wedding. As soon as he felt safe, he began to expose his true jealous, controlling self. It is also possible that Vicky closed her eyes to the obvious because she wanted to get married and thought he would change.

When we compromise our own needs and desires for fear of losing someone, we become the real loser. Our life becomes a façade, hiding our true self for fear of being rejected. When you compromise your wants and needs, you send out a message that says I don't count so go ahead and take advantage of me. I am weak and will cave in to your demands. Are you settling in your relationship or marriage because you believe you have no alternative? Did you establish any ground rules early in the relationship? If your expectations were never established before you became involved, then you have a real problem to solve. You may now be experiencing what happens when you love someone more than they love you.

Constantly suppressing your feelings and shoving them down deep inside is a sure recipe for resentment, anxiety and depression. I was always so afraid to say what I really felt for fear of being rejected or isolated. I love Steve Harvey's book, *Act Like a Lady Think Like a Man: What Men Really Think About Love, Relationships, Intimacy, and Commitment.* Steve says, *"When you're not aware that all men have plans, you're not placing requirements on him, and if you're not setting any ground rules, then you are essentially telling him that you're open for his rules."* Steve goes on to say that once he realizes he has complete control, you have given him a license to disrespect you. If you want to be treated like a princess, you need to establish your rules from the start!

Learn to rest in who you are without inwardly criticizing yourself for what you perceive as failure. Actually, what you are experiencing might not be failure at all but simply a learning and growing challenge. Stop being your own worst critic. If you feel you are not in the place you want to be, then work toward changing it. What is your biggest concern? Are you a chronic worrier or maybe you need to work on your critical nature? You and only you hold power over your desire to change.

I have read dozens and dozens of self-help books, attended seminars and counseling sessions, listened to motivational lectures and taken advice from trusted friends. I can tell you from my own experience that real change comes only when we are at peace with who we are and what we are at this present moment in time and space. Ridding yourself of fear and doubt will free your sub-conscious mind to be receptive to change. Resting in the present moment does not mean that this is where you want to stay forever. What it does do is help quell inner anxiety and frustration as you live day by day. Each moment moves us forward and each moment can change. As you learn to accept and embrace life in the moment, it actually brings a sense of control because you have made a conscious decision not to strive and run yourself to death on life's speeding treadmill!

Once you make that decision to stop striving, you will free your subconscious mind from turmoil and begin to reprogram your inner dialog that life is good and all is well. This new freedom will open up pathways from the Universe to speak to your soul and guide you on the path you want to be traveling. Once the fear is lifted, the course of action becomes clearer.

I shared in my previous book how I grew up in a dysfunctional home of violence. My father was extremely critical and quick to point out if my report card was not all A's like my sister Carol's. Because we never knew what would trigger anger, we were always on guard and fearful of innocently causing violent reactions. We were always living in an atmosphere of anticipation which in me led to inner panic and paranoia that something bad was going to happen. I have been years reprogramming my mind to stop the fearful thoughts. Thinking about a wonderful hike in the woods might instantly switch to being attacked by a bear. Imagining a peaceful ocean scene might end with a shark attack. I believe my good/bad thoughts wrapped around one event were a result of the mixed signals I experienced from my father.

Whenever I was sick, my father was always the one who brought in the chicken noodle soup and ginger ale on a TV tray and place it by the bed. He would drive us to school when it was below freezing, and I even remember him appearing at school unannounced and walking up to the teacher to inform her that he was born left-handed and so was his son. He told her he wanted her to stop trying to force my brother Chuck to write right-handed. With that, he turned and left. We were so proud and yet so scared. We might come home that same day and find him drunk and screaming and yelling at our mother.

Releasing this ingrained fear is still a work in progress but each day I spend time naming all the things I am thankful for in my life. I have always tried to overcome my fears. I wanted to scuba dive so badly but never had the courage to take dive lessons. I was shocked one Christmas when David, my husband, gave me a gift of scuba diving lessons. He loved to scuba dive and wanted me to share it with him. Now I had no excuse except my fear.

I went first to class lectures on how to use the dive gear and then came the pool dive training. I might add that I was the only woman in the class and the oldest. Both the dive master and the assistant dive master were chauvinist and did not in any way try to hide the fact. I was told by the assistant dive master that he would be right on me constantly to make sure I understood the instructions. The first thing we did was partner up, dive down and exchange breathing tubes. He was sure I would panic when I had to sit on the bottom of the pool, remove my mask, replace it and blow out the water. The more he challenged me, the more grit I determined to have.

The next step was to swim twelve laps of the pool without stopping. Of course, I was the only one who received a lecture. This time it was the dive master who said, "I don't know how good of a swimmer you are, but obviously you must know how to swim or you would not have joined this class. You have to complete the laps in order to go on the ocean dive." I stood there bristling enough to keep the adrenaline pumping to get me through the twelve laps. This was an Olympic sized pool, but was there any room for failure? NO!

The final test was the Key Largo 30-foot ocean dive. We had to dive three separate times to get certified and due to severe weather and rough seas our dive was cancelled twice. At the end of January, we were told no more cancellations. It was bitter cold even by Florida standards and I am 5'8" tall and weigh 120 pounds. This is significant as I was in danger of hypothermia. I was thankful they let David come along on the dive boat. We had minimal visibility during the dive and I could hardly see the instructor let alone my partner. I was fearful but determined as I had been through plenty with these yoyo guys and I was not going to allow them to scare me out of my certification.

I came up after the first dive and David saw me trembling and immediately poured warm water inside my wet suit. My teeth were chattering so violently I thought they might crumble. The instructor was watching and waiting for me to shout "uncle' but no chance! I jumped back in the water after the 20-minute wait. Now it was time to take off my mask, put it back on and blow out the water, then rescue my partner by giving him my breathing tube. Back to the dive boat for 20 more minutes. One more dive to go and in the water I went. Victory! I was elated and all I needed after that was a very hot bath.

What adventure are you desiring and yet fearing? Maybe it is time to look fear in the face and just jump in! Maybe you want to try white water rafting, a hot air balloon ride or sky diving. As I began writing this book, my friend Marilyn was in Costa Rica and I received an email describing her jungle adventure. Marilyn said, "I just did 16 zip- lines over canyons and through jungles. It was so thrilling! I just loved it as I sailed above the trees, hanging from a cable going up to 50 miles per hour." Wow, Marilyn! The next day, she was on her way to another zip-line excursion and while chatting with a couple on the bus, they said, "We were zip-lining yesterday and there was an older

Barbara Miller

women zip- lining alone. She was having a ball." Marilyn just smiled and then in unison they said, "Oh wow, it was you!"

Sounds like something I want to put on my bucket list! Most importantly, do not let the trauma of your past rob you of a fulfilling future. Was I fearful doing my dive training? You bet I was, but I wanted the experience more and the only way to accomplish it was to face my fear and jump in the water. Say yes to the challenges and adventures you want to experience!

A year after my dive training, David and I went to Cozumel, Mexico on vacation. We had found a dive master on line who took only small groups. I had been down a few times, once to 75 feet, and I did not like going that deep. Thirty-five feet was deep enough for me and this was the depth he advertised.

Upon arriving at the dock and observing the dilapidated conditions, I thought, oh no. Then I saw the dive master who was clearly out of the 60s, with dreadlocks down to his waist. I was ready to bolt; however, everything changed in an instant as more people arrived. They walked up and began hugging and kissing him and were expressing how much they had looked forward to diving with him again. Then to my joy I saw his *new* dive equipment and gave a deep sigh of relief.

Things were looking up until I got in the water. No matter how much weight they put on me, I kept bobbing back to the surface. The guide finally took my hand and pulled me down with him. He never let go of my hand for the entire dive and it turned into one of my most pleasurable adventures. He refused to let me wear gloves and made me touch certain plants and creatures that he knew we wouldn't harm and were safe. It was amazing as I came face to face with eels, snakes, lobster, and octopus and when a shark swam overhead, I was not scared!

What a miracle and what joy. David said he was jealous because I was seeing and experiencing underwater life and creatures and he spent all his time trying to see what we were looking at. What joy and excitement is awaiting you? Go out and conquer your fear like I did in my scuba diving lessons. Look fear straight in the face and walk right through it to the other side and jump in. Yes! We are no longer afraid.

"I have been absolutely terrified every moment of my life and I've never let it keep me from doing a single thing that I wanted to do." Georgia O'Keeffe

- I will not let fear own me.
- I will not be crippled by my fear.
- I will face my fear as I look to the God of the universe for strength and healing.
- I will remember my mantra: I am beautiful, I am strong, and I am a princess.

Dare to have the courage to step apart and view your own life. Is it the life you really want to be living? If not—why not? Are you willing to explore other possibilities or will you choose to stay stuck in the familiar? Only you can step out of your current situation and redesign your life. Seeking a new direction and leaving a familiar life for a new path takes tremendous courage. Ask yourself: *What will I gain if I leave my present marriage, job, home—what will I gain if I stay?*

"The unexamined life is not worth living." Plato

Barbara Miller

To be real is to be vulnerable—to speak our truth is to be vulnerable, and to examine and change our life path is to be vulnerable. However, the key to finding your true self is to look within, and in order to fully live your true self, you must go on a personal quest to find the real you.

"Courage is being scared to death—but still saddling up."
John Wayne

Chapter 2
DANCE OF INTENTION

"Most of us weren't trained to be creative. We were trained to be analytical, logical, detail-oriented, judgmental, and reasonable! Creativity comes out of unreasonableness. It comes out of imagination, intuition, humor, vision, music, and nonjudgement."
Cheryl Gilman, author

Healing can come in many forms and recognizing inner pain and past hurts is the first step toward healing our soul. Maybe it is too painful to face all the buried hurts at once so just take them one by one. The important thing is that you face them. Make peace with your pain. The most difficult forgiving I ever had to do was forgiving my father but the cost of anger and sadness was too much weight to carry around. It was a long journey toward healing and even now I find myself remembering and asking why? Why couldn't you love your family enough to seek help? Why did you treat us that way? We were good kids and just wanted your love, not violence and threats. Then the universe answered back and said, "It was the best he could do. He simply did not have the strength or resources to challenge his own inner pain."

I remember vividly coming home and rushing in to announce that I had just been given a position at the Brown City Savings Bank through a co-op program at my high school. This would count as credits toward my graduation requirements. It was my senior year and I would attend classes in the morning and work afternoons at the bank. I was ecstatic! I remember walking in the kitchen after school, excited to tell my great news; however, I had not anticipated the shunning I would receive from both my parents. My mother went back to cooking dinner and my father turned and went outside. My father did not speak to me for two weeks and my mother remained a cool distance. When I finally asked her what was going on and why Dad was not speaking to me, she said, "Your dad never expected you to get that job. Nobody in the family has ever had a job like that and he believes now you will think you are too good for the rest of us."

I had been hurt by many things my entire life but I don't think up to that point that anything had ever hurt me so deeply. I was astounded at my mother's lack of support, but I knew that much of her response stemmed from not having graduated from high school and simply struggling to survive each day. To this day, the memory of that time in my life is still painful.

Carrying pain and past hurts will take its toll on your mental and physical health. A client shared this story of inner anger and rage that she had kept locked up for years.

Barbara Miller

Sharon's Story

I was molested by an uncle when I was a young girl. I still have difficulty with the rage towards my mother for leaving me with my grandparents sometimes for a week. I also feel anger because I was unable to tell her what was happening to me as I was ashamed and scared.

My uncle would lure me alone and sexually molest me. My grandmother seemed oblivious to what was happening and she had such a mean disposition that I was afraid to tell, and he bribed me with candy and money. One night to my terror I awakened to find myself in his bed. He had carried me from my bed to his and for the first time I felt terrified of being raped. He held his hand over my mouth and became more aggressive. I struggled and said I would tell my dad and began to cry. He gave me a dollar and made me promise not to tell and said he would never do it again.

I never told my mother until I was an adult and her response to me was, "Well, at least you never got hurt." I was so shocked that she did not express any outrage or empathy whatsoever. I thought she would apologize to me for leaving me in such a volatile situation, but her excuse was that she did not know things like that happened so it was not her fault. I felt guilty and dirty all over again and I wanted to scream at my mother, "Why didn't you protect me and why didn't you tell me I could always come to you if I was afraid?"

I am still afraid and I cannot seem to trust anyone. I have been in several relationships and eventually they all leave because of my mistrust and anger. I am so lonely and desperately want to get married and have a family, but I just cannot seem to know how to let go of my past.

Instead, I swallowed my anger and shoved it down deeper and deeper until it began to erupt in my adult life in fits of rage. I had hoped my mother would sympathize and say how sorry she was and express regret that I was traumatized, but instead I got nothing from her at all. I have found a wonderful counselor and am still working through my pain. At least now I have someone I can talk to and hold my hand when I cry and scream and struggle to let go of the past.

My heart went out to Sharon as she shared this heartbreaking story. I do feel that seeking help through a counselor was the only way Sharon could be released from the ghosts of her past. She told me that what she really wanted to do was scream at her uncle but he had died and there was no way she could ever confront him. Sharon's mother was also no longer living and she found herself caught in the nightmare of her past and no one to blame for her anger.

If underlying anger is eating away at you like a cancer on the inside, you can be sure it will manifest itself on the outside. You may experience fits of rage as Sharon did, or lash out at loved ones, drivers, cashiers or anyone who gets in your way. You must seek professional help. Suppressed anger is a vicious companion, leaving you isolated from the very ones you love the most. Being molested, threatened or rejected early in life can lead to feelings of unworthiness later in life and create a deep sense of insecurity.

There are no replays on our past, there is no one calling "Cut!" Let's take it from the top again! We just get one dry run for the actual scene of our past and then we play it and play it until we drive ourselves crazy with regrets. You need to "cut," then turn around and look ahead. Stop looking back, it is a done deal! Don't work and sweat in your mind in an attempt to change your past, it simply cannot be done. Take a look at the good part though; we can direct our own future with our thoughts and desires. We can come into perfect alignment with the great Universal Mind and control our own destiny.

If we deleted all the data from our computer, we would then have nothing more than an empty box. The same is true for our brain. If we deleted every past experience, whether past hurts, pain, loss, fear, happiness, joy, we would in fact delete our personality, the very essence of who we are. The difference with change is that we focus on the positive. Start by becoming aware of negative thoughts and patterns and how you react to them. What is your inner dialog? Only in becoming aware of your negative thoughts can you effect change. Do not think on the negative or what you don't want, but realize that our life experiences move us toward what we do want. All aspects of our lives are learning and developing processes. Allowing negative memories to live on in our mind simply reinforces their energy. Pay attention and recognize the space you have allowed them to occupy.

If you believe you want to change your negative beliefs but feel helpless to do so, ask yourself why? You may be selling yourself short and perhaps you do not need to change anything. For instance, I was raised in a church that preached condemnation and sin. Everything was a sin. Dancing was a sin, along with going to movies, drinking and smoking. Sex was considered dirty and only allowed for procreation. Even attending a church of another denomination or doctrine was a sin. It wasn't until I learned that our pastor was asked by the elders of the church to step down for having an affair with a pastor's wife from another church that I began to question the doctrine of guilt. I was at the impressionable age of thirteen when I realized that I had been taught lies by a mere man who could not even control his own life.

I am not saying that overindulgence in some of his list of sins could not be destructive to a life; I am saying I was taught fear, condemnation and guilt! So much of the screaming from the pulpit of our need to repent or burn in hell was a lie and I did not need to live my life condemning myself. I can still remember the sadness I felt as the church voted to release the pastor from his leadership position. I looked at his wife and felt her pain.

What is Your Deepest Intention?

What are you expecting in your life? What self-imposed obstacles have you allowed your mind to accept as truth and what past beliefs are holding you back? It is time to break loose from limiting old patterns and begin setting new standards for yourself as you start moving forward to a new satisfying life. Your value comes from the King of the Universe and that makes you a *princess*. Being related to the King of the Universe makes us heirs to His estate. Wow, that is powerful so stand up tall and proud, my beautiful princesses, as we walk together in the knowledge of who we are and who we belong to.

While having lunch with a friend who is a licensed clinical therapist, I shared with her about the negative thoughts I was having continually. They just never seemed to let up and I could not understand why I was incapable of silencing them. It was a constant barrage of fearful 'what ifs' that never happened except in my mind. Some kind of tragedy was always about to happen and I had to find a way to stop it or warn someone of impending doom.

She explained that because I had grown up having to be constantly on guard and ready for what might happen in our household, my brain had become conditioned to be on high alert, to warn me to run and hide on a moment's notice. She compared it to our ancestor's flight or fight instincts when being threatened by a wild animal. The anxiety this causes for a child year after year takes its toll until the brain begins to recognize that these invading thoughts are not real. The thoughts will continue and keep picking up momentum until you recognize them for what they are and dismiss the intrusion.

I know this sounds way too simplistic, but really concentrate on the fact that you have been lied to and these thoughts have no power over you! The ego is feeding the self a worthless barrage of dialog in order to keep a grip on control. The ego's biggest fear is that you will discover its weakness. The ego knows that all you have to do to call its bluff is to calmly acknowledge its presence and tell it you are aware that it is feeding you lies to keep you fearful and off balance. State that you are no longer going to tolerate or believe these lies. Yes, you may have to mentally repeat this scenario dozens of times throughout each day but eventually the ego will give up the charade, knowing it has been discovered and exposed for what it really is–a liar and deceiver.

When negative inner dialog takes over, step back from yourself like another person and ask yourself: *Is this really true?* Chances are you will recognize it for what it really is. It is your ego desperately attempting to keep control! Each time you challenge your ego and begin to release negative thoughts, give thanks and tell your mind how happy you are for your new-found freedom. This is also the time to do mindfulness meditation by expressing love and gratitude to your Higher Power. The more you focus on love, gratitude and forgiveness, the more reinforced your mind will be toward the changes you are initiating.

Try not to be too hard on yourself. The first step toward wholeness is being happy in who you really are. If there is something about yourself that you do not like, then change it or get someone to help you. Surround yourself with positive people and read positive uplifting material. Meditate and keep your mind focused on all things good in your life. Imagine yourself standing on the very edge of the earth. All you can see of the earth in your mind's eye is the slight curve you are standing on. You see all the stars and heavenly bodies and sense you are part of all there is or ever was. Well, guess what? You are! Now stretch out your hands and imagine a great white light coming towards you like a laser beam. It's coming straight at you and is now flooding your entire body with pure white light. Now imagine being cleansed and freed from all negative thoughts and past hurts that have been plaguing you. Allow your negative thoughts to enter your mind's eye and then release them to the pure white light. Nothing dark and negative can stand this pure white light. Accept this light and let it flood every atom in your body.

In my previous book, *You Lost Your Marriage Not Your Life*, I write about the little child within each of us who wants only to be loved and feel cherished and safe. She wants to dance in rhythm with the Universe and be embraced and told she is beautiful and valuable; that she is a *princess*. We ask the question, "How do we find her, where is she? How can I nurture the child within when I cannot love the adult without?"

Estelle's Story

I was at the grocery store with my mother when a very handsome man walked by. He glanced at me and smiled as he walked by. I was fifteen and looked older, but I did not think much of it as obviously he was an older man. My mother began to lecture me and remind me that I looked more like eighteen and I should avoid eye contact with men as they may think I am attempting to be seductive. When I declared that I did not look at him deliberately, she insisted that I had enticed him.

The next time I had such an encounter with my mother was over a man who worked for my father. I was sixteen and Richard was about thirty years old and always left his car parked at our house and rode to work with my father. I was very upset one day as I had to go to work and my mother had an early appointment and was not available to drive me. I was asking my father what

I should do when Richard said, "Here, take my keys and use my car as we will be gone all day."

When my mother found out that night, she was furious! I was accused of sexually luring older men. Then she decided that I was sneaking out to see him. None of it was true. When my eighteenth birthday came, she announced that I would not be getting anything for my birthday. When I asked about my usual birthday cake, she said, "No, do you really think I am going to bake you a cake after your behavior?"

I always wanted my mother's approval and she never complimented me or encouraged me. I always felt unworthy of love and still struggle, seeking approval and pleasing people. My mother is now old and needs help and I try to do what I can, but she still cannot hug me or thank me. She still looks at me with contempt. I don't think she ever loved or wanted me.

Fear keeps us from change and from finding out who we really are. Fear blocks us from going back and facing old habits and patterns. Can it really help or will it just cause more pain? I used to check out Cinderella from the Bookmobile each time it came to my school. Finally, after the third time, the gentle Bookmobile librarian encouraged me to choose another book so some other little girl could have a chance to read it. I was painfully disappointed as it had become the fantasy of my inner self. I dreamed of Cinderella every day as I carefully turned the pages. The librarian led me over to the fairytale section and helped me choose another book. This was when I first learned of all the early fairytales like Thumbelina, The Princess and the

Pea, Snow White, and Sleeping Beauty, but Cinderella was forever my favorite fairytale.

I simply could not get enough of reading fairytales. I would dream of crystal lakes sparkling with diamonds, and being transformed into a beautiful princess with a gorgeous gown and jewel-encrusted crown, and being carried on the back of a splendid white swan.

Looking at fairytale books with their elaborate images fostered my creativity. Much of my thought life was fantasizing about how to create beauty. Aunt Lillian, my mother's sister, used to send a box of play clothes each summer for my sister Carol and me when we were young girls. We were so excited to open the box and see what Aunt Lillian had created just for us. She always sent the left-over scrap material so we could make matching doll clothes.

We learned to sew on the old pedal sewing machine. I was too small to reach the pedal while sitting so I learned to sew standing up. It was such fun to sew fashions for my doll that matched mine. I loved to pretend that I was a beautiful princess. It was an escape from the constant fear I was exposed to on a daily basis. However, it would be many more years before I would learn that God's word says we are crowned with glory and honor, and I truly am and always have been a *princess*.

Imagination

When I was in sixth grade, we were instructed by our school teacher to write a play that we would work on together. We would perform our play for our mothers on parent-teacher day. We were all so excited and were given permission to hold meetings in the girl's coat room. It was a one-room school house and boys and girls had a coat room. It was a big deal for the boys to be allowed in the girl's private room and they always entered while sheepishly looking around. We all sat on the floor to discuss ideas for our play. I came up with some ideas that the others liked so I was given the leadership role of our little group of six. This was the total number of fifth and sixth grade students.

We were all excited as we rehearsed and found costumes. The hardest costume to come up with was a costume for our giant mouse. One of the girls had one-piece red flannel pajamas that would be her mouse costume. I had written a fairytale about a princess, prince, and wicked witch. The day finally came and we proudly put on our play for our mothers.

It had never once occurred to me that my mother would not like our play. I rode home with my mother after school and was immediately confronted about the play. My mother demanded to know who had written that horrible play with girls crawling around in red flannel pajamas. I mumbled, "She was a mouse and that was her costume." My mother continued, "Well, your teacher should have never allowed you kids to put on that play, it was so embarrassing." "Momma, I wrote that play and the teacher liked it and so did all the kids." I was 11 years old and something in me died. From that day forward, my imagination could only stay in my mind and I became more careful about sharing my thoughts with anyone. My imagination would emerge many years later and reveal to me that my heart had held my deepest and dearest intentions in safe keeping. They were still there in my inner sanctum.

God was good when he gave us imagination. Beautiful poetry, paintings and books all blossomed from someone's imagination. All the roads we travel in this life help to shape who we are today. Our current circumstances might seem impossible to bear, but God promises that he will give us the support and strength we need to meet the challenges of today. Don't worry about what others think about you; it is what you think that defines who you are. Take a realistic inventory; call it a Discovery Inventory. Examine your strengths and gifts. No two people have the same knowledge and talents. Just look at yourself and resist the urge to compare to others.

My husband and I were out to dinner one evening with friends. I got up and went to the ladies' room to powder my nose. I noticed a woman watching me as I applied my lipstick. She said, "Could I use your makeup? I have been watching you and you are so pretty; if I could use your makeup maybe I could look like you. I don't like how I look and always want to look like someone else." First of all, I was astounded that she would even ask a stranger to use their makeup and second, she really believed that in using my makeup she could look like me! I stopped and studied her for a few seconds, searching for the right words. I could see she obviously had serious issues and I did not want to hurt her. I finally responded and said, "No, you cannot use my makeup. I never share my makeup with anyone and even if you could look just like me, you would still be you. You need to learn to love yourself and your own particular look. Learn to be the best you possibly can and accept your own individual self."

Joel Osteen writes in *Your Best Life Now Journal*, *"You can dare to be happy with who you are right now and accept yourself, faults and all."*

How do we develop a new way of thinking and how can we retrain our mind when all it knows is negative thinking? Like attracts like, so if we allow negative, disparaging thoughts to keep us fearful, it is like feeding and nurturing what you really want to get rid of. It is like feeding a stray animal and then wondering why it won't go home. Stop feeding and nurturing your negative thoughts and starve them out with powerful reinforced thoughts of praise and thanksgiving. It takes time to retrain your brain as it is accustomed to a certain way of thinking, and will not take you seriously at first. You must be diligent in your commitment to change your pattern of thinking and accept only positive thoughts. Keep your Princess Diary with you at all times, and when old unwanted thoughts start trespassing, write them in your diary and put a red line right through them. They need to be replaced immediately with all the qualities that make you the wonderful beautiful princess you truly are.

It is important to align your self-image with the power of positive thinking. The two must be going down the same path in order to create change. This is determined only by you and the goals you have set for yourself. We can intellectually tell ourselves that we are going to change, but unless we willfully decide and practice change coming into alignment with our intellect, it will never happen.

"Take the opportunity to learn from your mistakes; find the cause of your problem and eliminate it. Don't

try to be perfect; just be an excellent example of being human." Tony Robbins

What are your deepest desires and how do you intend to manifest them? Without a burning desire and definiteness of purpose, you will flounder and easily lose sight of your goals. You must have a clearly defined intention as to what you want to accomplish in your life. Is it personal change you want to focus on or perhaps a job change or relocation? Whatever it is, you must clearly define it and keep it planted foremost in your mind. You must come to know and nurture this intended change so clearly that you believe you are already living your desire. Being consciously aware brings power to your intention to reach your goals.

If you are not consciously orchestrating and directing the life you want for yourself, you will continue on the same path you have always trodden. Your intention for change must become a cultivated habit. Imagine planting a garden and not fertilizing or watering it. If you neglect to weed your garden, the weeds will ultimately choke out your entire desired outcome and it will die. This is exactly what will happen to your goals if they are not watered and fertilized on a daily basis.

If you are on *"the downward path to nowhere"* and are always struggling to climb back up only to travel the same path again and again, maybe it is time to find a new route to your destination. If you keep taking your path to nowhere, you will always arrive where you have always been—stuck and discouraged. Get off center; the center is the path you have always taken.

I love to visit Mackinaw Island in upper Michigan. The island is very hilly and everywhere you go, it takes effort to climb the steep hills. However, there is a flat road at the bottom that circles the entire island. You can rent a bike or walk with no effort and the view is breathtaking. Many people never discover the flat road at the bottom because they are too busy climbing up and down the hills. If you are still taking the *downward path to nowhere,* you might try making a quantum shift to the right or left and walking the flat road.

For your deepest intention and goals for your life to take action, they must be deeply planted in your mind and brought to the conscious forefront daily. Every single day, read your goals out loud and do something—anything that moves you closer toward your intended goal.

Be careful where you seek advice. You may actually ask someone for an opinion and get far more than you bargained for. They may not understand your intention or motive and insult you in a way that undermines your confidence. Remember: only you know fully what you are trying to accomplish and asking for advice from a friend or family member may set you back and discourage you from accomplishing your goals.

I remember many years ago I was preparing a speech on tape to send to a company I wanted to speak for and I trusted a woman to listen to my talk and give an opinion. She called me later and said, "Whatever you do, do not send them that tape. I know exactly the type of delivery they are looking for in a speech. After listening to your tape, I can assure you that they will not accept this. I am trying to protect you from embarrassing yourself." I mumbled a confused "Thank you," hung up and immediately burst into tears. I did not make any attempt to get on the speaker's circuit for this company for six months. I had been unprepared for the insensitivity of this woman and the sad part is that I allowed her to intimidate me from doing something that I really wanted to do.

I was at the pool one day with a close friend and she shared with me how she had accepted a position on the board for one of the women's clubs affiliated with the company I had intended to send my speech to. I told her a little of what had happened and she asked to have the tape. I was fearful but I gave it to her despite my apprehension. Two days later, she called and expressed how meaningful my message was to her and she would love to have me speak at her club. I spoke for that company for five years!

Be careful of the "dream robbers." I was thrown off course because I allowed another woman to assassinate my dreams. Do not allow this to happen to you by remembering who you are. "I am beautiful, I am strong, and I am a princess!"

If you have a message struggling to find its way out, don't fight it. Take a few deep breaths and release it to the universe. The universe knows what you feel and what you want and will always work with you, not against you. It is your greatest ally. You know the real you and if writing a book and speaking your truth is your life's goal, then grab your pen and let the ink flow. Never be afraid to trust in yourself and the miracles of the Universe.

- What do you really want for your life—your deepest intention?

- Is your mind bombarding you with negative dialog?
- What action are you taking to bring your intellect into alignment with your desires?
- Is underlying anger or fear preventing you from moving forward?

If you are struggling with answers to the above questions, I encourage you to seek professional help. Life is too valuable to miss out on all the miracles just waiting for you to receive.

"All the answers you seek lie within. Daily, in moments of quiet, ask yourself for the direction you seek, and look for the answers in your feelings and intuitions."

Mike Dooley

Chapter 3
DANCE OF GOALS

"I will not start any sentence with the words "I can't." If I do, my mind will accept it as so, and then I won't be able to accomplish my goals. Instead, I will tell myself, "I can," or, "I will." In this way, success will come to me. Suzanne Somers

Have you considered your personal goals and written them down? If you are only thinking about your inner desires and simply letting them sit there in your mind, then that is where they are likely to stay. Thinking about our goals is indeed the first step but outlining them with pen and paper breathes more life into them. It is like starting to build a house. First, we envision exactly what we want our home to look like and then we sketch up a plan. We work the plan until it rings true to what we want in our new home and then we have blueprints drawn up. Then, assuming we have secured the lot, we start the building project. We follow the building progress every day until finally we are gazing at our new home.

This is exactly how our goals progress to reality, by taking action to build our dreams. If we do not take necessary steps towards our goals, our mind does not take us seriously. I hear this story frequently: "I always wanted to write a book, but I just could never find the time." When I ask them about their outline, they say, "Oh, that's all in my head." Well, guess what. That is where it will likely stay. Wishing will not produce a written manuscript, and without a burning desire to hold that book in your hand, it will never happen! Our actions are reflected by what we believe. If you believe you can accomplish your goals and physically move towards them, you will succeed! Only you can determine your motivation to reach your goals.

My son-in-law Glenn is a builder and an expert at remodeling houses. His creative genius is impressive as he meticulously draws up plans and then studies his plans to determine if there might be a better way to achieve his ultimate goal. The drawings must have order and flow and must make sense. After careful consideration, he may deem it necessary to change his plans or adjust them to attain the desired outcome. Once he feels assured that he has created the best possible plan, he begins construction. He has the final finished project laid out in detail before ordering material and starting construction. We have all seen building projects that were a nightmare in design because they were not thought through clearly. The same principles apply to setting our goals for a successful life.

Consider what you could do to change your current behavior to bring you one step closer to realizing your dreams. I used to get up at 5:00 a.m. to write before getting ready for work. I often took my notebook with me in case I had thoughts I needed to write down before they escaped me. I just kept reminding myself that I wanted a new career and it was writing, public speaking and conducting self-help seminars for women. I believed my book was the catalyst that would help bring it all together. It never would have happened had I not had a burning desire to hold my printed book in my hand. Whether I was on our boat or on an airplane, I was reading and writing with profound passion!

Do not expect other people to understand what you are trying to accomplish. Only you see your life dreams in your mind's eye—not them. Don't become discouraged if you are not getting the support you want from family and friends, just keep your focus and follow your dreams. Try not to beat yourself up with disparaging thoughts. It is a normal reaction to criticism to allow self-doubt to creep in and activate the inner voice that says, "What makes you think you can accomplish that or reach so high?" That is the time you need to take out your *Positive Thoughts Journal* and reread your goals to remind yourself that you are worthy and capable of accomplishing anything you set your mind to.

"Don't let the noise of other's opinions drown out your own inner voice, and most important, have the courage to follow your heart and intuition. They somehow already know what you truly want to become. Everything else is just secondary."

Steve Jobs

I was having lunch one day with a group of women when one of them asked me what I did for a living. I replied that I was writing a book. She turned her head to the side and rolled her eyes. Her actions were obvious indications of her thoughts which were—please give me a break; everybody is going to write a book. I was so embarrassed by her demoralizing look but I just smiled and said to myself, 'Just watch me, sweetheart!' Don't let people undermine your plans. Her attitude just fueled my determination to hold my book and personally place it in her hands. Which I did! The one thing I knew for sure was that I was writing a book, not that I was thinking about writing a book. She could not look inside my brain and see my goals and dreams, but it didn't change the fact that they were there. No one can totally understand you—but you.

You are the one in charge of your future so don't allow anyone else to take over that role. Your life dance belongs to you and only you! Sinclair Lewis said the right words, *"It is impossible to discourage the real writers—they don't give a damn what you say, they're going to write."*

Another example is while visiting with a friend one day and sharing my goals and dreams, I noticed that she remained silent and started looking down. Finally, she said, "Barbara, everyone would like to accomplish goals but most never write a book. It is extremely difficult to write and promote a book. Are you certain you want to devote the time and effort it would take for such a lofty goal?" I was stunned and disappointed at her unwillingness to support and encourage me and I will confess her negative words and behavior hurt me deeply. However, I had learned a lot from Napoleon Hill, author of *Think and Grow Rich*. I had clearly defined goals and definiteness of purpose. I was on a mission and I knew absolutely that I would write my book! Focus on already being there, not on how to get there. This puts you in total alignment with your dreams and goals.

Don't let people snatch away your power by "zapping" you. We have all been zapped at some point. You know the feeling when you are chatting and sharing and the person hits you in the gut with her mean-spirited remark. You sit there stunned by her poison remark arrow zap, and she goes on without missing a beat. This is not a person who is loving and gracious and you may want to consider giving her your own zap—called the disappearing zap of your magic wand.

Mike Dooley author of *Infinite Possibilities* says, *"This is not a Universe that compassionately watches you like a doting parent but a Universe with superpowers that are yours to leverage."* My friend had no idea that I had leveraged the Universe to help me accomplish my goals and I knew I could trust my heart's desire to this all knowing-all loving Universe which never tires of working on my behalf. My desire to see others holding and reading my finished book drove me to reach my goal. Only you know what you want and when you blend that knowledge with a burning desire, nothing can stop you from victory!

To get the same degree of clarity you must have to set your goals, it must be blended with equal parts emotion or enthusiasm. Without clearly defined goals and a definite plan to attain them, you will be like a ship lost at sea without a navigation map. My husband David had a harrowing adventure at sea while attempting to drive our boat from Ft. Lauderdale, Florida to Naples, Florida. He had to navigate through the Florida Keys to get from the east coast to the west coast. His GPS was not working properly and his depth finder was old and not accurate. He went aground on a sand bar. After numerous attempts trying to get off the sand bar, he heard the voice on the radio ordering him to stop his engines as he was close to a coral reef. They sent out a tow boat which successfully towed him off the sandbar but as soon as he got started, he went a short distance and hit another sandbar. This time when they sent the tow boat back, David had them tow him completely out of the area. Eight thousand dollars later, he was on his way to Naples, Florida.

It certainly would have been much cheaper to have had a better GPS and an up-to-date depth finder. I guess you know exactly what he did the day after he arrived in Naples. He went shopping for the best GPS and most accurate depth finder he could find! Also, had he checked in with the bridge captain before he started his fateful journey, they would have told him it was shallow ahead and to take a different route. David had a goal to get from the east coast to the west coast but he had not mapped out the proper route to accomplish that goal.

The same is true about manifesting our dreams without set goals and a plan to reach them. Do you love what you are doing with a burning desire to see it to fruition? If not, why not? You surely do not want to wind up aground on some sandbar. My actions were continually in line with my goal for my book. If you *wait till the midnight hour* to make your first move towards accomplishing your heart's desire, chances are you'll just yawn and go to bed. Maybe it is time to get moving and take charge before life passes you by. Learn to live your life with purpose and without fear of what others think by remembering that your thoughts order the events of your world. Peggy McColl, author of *Your Destiny Switch*, says, *"Don't talk yourself out of doing what you're meant to do just because you feel scared for some reason or don't know what turn to make next."*

Rachel's Story

Stan, my husband, was in medical school studying to be a dentist when we met. He was different from other men I had dated, he seemed sure of himself and what he wanted from life. I loved being around him and we started dating almost immediately. I had just come out of a disastrous relationship. I had dated this man through high school and finally broke up with him because he tried to coerce me into having sex. I kept trying to explain that I was fearful of getting pregnant and it was against my religion to have sex out of wedlock. I wanted to go to college so I broke up with him and he was so upset he joined the army. I was devastated that he just up and left without warning so I determined in my mind that I was not going to lose another man because I refused to have sex.

Stan was so much fun while we were dating and even though I wasn't totally in love with him, I decided not to keep refusing his sexual advances. I had already lost the man I thought I would marry because of sex. It was not long before I became pregnant and I was terrified to have to tell him. He said he did not want to get married, but took responsibility for my condition. He said, "If it does not work out, we will just get a divorce." I went into the marriage knowing we were not in love.

After we had been married for a few months, we began having financial problems as I was unable to work at this point. He was forced to quit medical school and find a full-time job. He was extremely bitter about having to make this decision, and took his anger out on me and the baby. He started drinking and

49

coming home later each night. Our nights became a battle ground of arguing and accusing one another for our predicament. I was bitter because I had only been able to attend two years of college and he was angry at having to quit med school. Our baby was the innocent victim caught up in the turmoil of two unhappy parents. I decided that I was going to leave him and discovered I was pregnant again. My first baby was only a few months old and now I knew for sure that I was trapped in the life I had helped create with no way out.

Our life became a predictable pattern of him coming in drunk and screaming at me and the children for ruining his life. Twenty years went by and the pattern never changed. I finally filed for divorce and much to my surprise he cried and begged me not to leave him. I stood there with no expression on my face and void of any feelings as I watched this pathetic man who had made our lives miserable and alienated our children. We had been his batting board as he ranted and screamed at us for what he felt he had lost in life and now I wanted nothing from him. I packed my bags and walked out of my home and into a new life and this time I would choose more wisely.

Stan had made me suffer by blaming me for all of our problems and I finally came to realize that he made his own choice to quit medical school. I believe that if he wanted it bad enough, he would have found a way to get it. The guilt I felt all those years took its toll on me as I took responsibility for getting pregnant and causing him to miss out on his dream. I had looked to him to find fulfillment in my life, but it only brought more emptiness. I don't know exactly what made me see that he was just using me and the kids as excuses for his own lack of determination, I just know one day I stood up to him and told him it was time to point his finger the other way—at himself. I was leaving him and now he would have plenty of time to decide what to do with the life he had left.

I had the pleasure of meeting Rachael just after she graduated from nursing school. She told me, "I always believed that being married and having a family would provide all the love and happiness I needed. All my life I was willing to take the blame and responsibility for someone else's loss and disappointments, but not anymore. I now look to myself to be accountable to me and I have never been happier in my entire life."

Who are you surrounding yourself with? Do they support and encourage you or constantly put you down? If you make relationships your life, you will always be unhappy because people will let you down. They have good and bad days just like you and if you need uplifting on one of their bad days, they might choose the wrong words and disappoint you. You must create a life that gives many layers and talents apart from others. Find ways to explore your personal gifts and passions, and don't depend on others to validate you. You, along with the King of the Universe, are enough!

Are you sabotaging your own goals by constantly verbalizing the negative aspects by including 'but what if' or 'if only' or 'maybe someday'? Your words must be in close alignment with your thoughts because if they are not, you are simply telling your brain that you do not think you can accomplish your goals. Start speaking words of power—worthy words.

Remember our mantra from, *You Lost Your Marriage Not Your Life: "I am beautiful, I am strong, and I am a princess."*

Your words are an extension of your thoughts and if you are reprogramming your mind with positive affirmations, then your spoken words should fall into alignment. To give life to your dreams, you must believe you are living your dreams already. When sending out thoughts to the Universe, be certain they are the positive ones. Always send out what you want to come back to you. Think of your thoughts like a boomerang. When you throw it out there, it always comes back to you. If, for instance, you want to attract the man of your dreams, begin envisioning what he should look like, how you would like him to treat you, what hobbies he should have to coincide with yours, and even his eating habits. List everything that you want to fall in alignment with your needs and desires. Are you verbally bashing men by saying things like 'all men are jerks'; 'men cannot commit'; 'you can't trust men'; or 'there are no good men out there'? If this is what you are thinking and actually telling others, you will attract exactly this type of man or *no man* at all. Dr. Wayne Dyer, in his new book, *Excuses Begone: How to Change Lifelong, Self-Defeating Thinking Habits*, tells us, *"The new biology says that there's an energy field surrounding, and contained within all your cells, and this field is influenced by your beliefs."*

Describe the man you want with passion and believe he is out there, just waiting for the right moment to walk into sight. Believe he is already manifested and you are just being introduced. See him smiling and smell his own distinct scent. Start by saying positive words like, 'the man of my dreams is

awesome, handsome, intelligent, and fun loving and generous.'
He dotes on me like I am a princess; he loves candlelight dinners
and fine wine, and he loves long walks. He is my *prince
charming*. You get the point—then give back thanks to the
Universe for revealing your perfect man.

Your perfect man may have totally different attributes than
mine. Maybe you like hiking or motorcycles or working on
antique cars, the important point is that you must visualize and
state what it is in a man that you want. I loved David's scent, it
melted right into me. There is definitely a primal instinct in all
of us that draws us to another. Take for instance, Al Pacino in
Scent of a Woman. Even though he had mastered the various
scents of perfume, I am certain it was more the scent of the
woman and not the perfume that drew him.

We all have written within us a life source that seeks our
highest good toward happiness and security. When your daily
thought life or mental picture of yourself is based on
unhappiness, guilt and failure, then you will invite more of the
same. The only way to change mental pictures that keep flashing
in your brain is to create new habits in the way you think and
act. Many of our daily routines are nothing more than habits and
these habits are on autopilot. Habits can be changed by
visualizing and creating daily habits of what you would really
like your life to be. Perhaps you might want to think about
someone you admire and practice mirroring them. Steve G.
Jones, life coach and hypnotist, teaches that if we mirror
someone we want to emulate, and do it consistently, that new
image will become anchored in our brain.

We are the only life source on the planet that can choose our goals. We can create anything we can imagine in our minds. Our mind is our servant and will serve us in the manner we have programmed it. Every single experience you have had is stored in your brain and in order for change to take place; you must believe there is a need for change. If the picture you have of yourself is based on not being good enough or unworthy, then change it. Resist negative statements about you like, *I don't have a life*. I cringe when women say this to me. If you don't have a life, then get one! Once you get your own life and begin to like your own company, you will then clear the stage for the *right* man to enter.

Begin to see yourself as happy, creative and successful. Seeing yourself accomplishing your end goal will provide a target. Once you have your desired outcome set securely in your mind, your success instincts will take over and work on your behalf. Focus on the arrow hitting the bull's eye. The picture or goal you have placed in your mind must be in total alignment with your thoughts. Change only comes to us when we see it already happening and act accordingly. If you could custom design the life you have always wanted, what would it look like? Perhaps you are happy with your life exactly as it is and have no desire to change anything. Only you know your deepest intention and what it would take to make your heart sing. Focus your efforts forward from this day toward your goals, not backward to your past.

I love to go on long walks and use that time to visualize and meditate. Perhaps you can only visualize by lying down and deep breathing with your eyes closed. It really does not matter which relaxation technique you use as long as it is quiet and you can focus on your goal without effort or strain. Our conscious mind actually programmed our unconscious mind much like a computer is programmed. We import or upload information and it is stored for future use. When we overload our computer, everything slows down until we sort through stored data and, with the click of a mouse, hit the delete key. Even though this seems simplistic when compared to the human personality, it is actually quite similar. We spend our entire lives dumping data or experiences into our brain and it holds the history of our lives! By changing your old self-defeating thoughts and habits and replacing them with new goals, it is like hitting the delete key.

Our thoughts are so powerful; it is like tossing a ball high in the air. Does it disappear into infinity? No, it comes back to you and so do your thoughts and words, so choose them wisely and zero in on their magic!

- Do you have a clear mental picture of what you want for your life?
- Are your personal gifts in alignment with your goals?
- Are you connected to loving friends and family who support and the goal you have set for your life?
- Do you have a target to shoot for?
- Do you visualize and program yourself for success?
- Do you believe in the possibility of change?

The answers to your life are held within you. They are just waiting to unfold and reveal themselves. Sometimes a lull in our plans is simply the Universe busy orchestrating the circumstances to allow your dreams to come to fruition.

Barbara Miller

> *"Somewhere out in this audience may even be someone who will one day follow in my footsteps, and preside over the White House as the President's spouse. I wish him well."* Barbara Bush, First Lady, Wellesley College Commencement

Chapter 4
DANCE OF SUCCESS

"Visualize this thing you want. See it, feel it, believe in it. Make your mental blueprint and begin." Robert Collier

We are wired to be creative by the greatest creative genius of all time, the Master Creator of the Universe. I love to entertain at Christmas and we always host a festive Christmas party for our friends. In preparation for this gala event, I fuss and adorn our home with beautiful Christmas decorations that I have collected over the years. I search through my cookbooks and choose which hors d'oeuvres to serve. I review my guest list to make certain I have not forgotten anyone. Two days before the party I shop, cook, bake and then clean the house and worry if I missed something. My husband David helps in any way he can, but I dive into this annual open house as though my life depended on it. However, once the day arrives and the doorbell rings, I take a deep breath and let the celebration begin! I have accomplished all I can possibly do and it is now time to let it all go and enjoy!

You may think this is a strange analogy in relationship to how our brain is wired, but it is really quite simple. I did all my worrying, planning, preparing and frantic running around but once the guests began to arrive, I was free to put all of my efforts aside and enjoy my guests. I had given much thought regarding how I wanted the evening to go. I had prepared accordingly to provide a successful festive party and now it was time to release that stress and enjoy myself. I no longer had to work and strive to control the situation, just enjoy the outcome.

Once you have made a decision and prepared accordingly, stop stressing over the outcome. Another example is planning a trip. We research and discuss different possibilities, then think about where we want to go and how we intend to get there. After weighing all the pros and cons, we sleep on it and finally make our decision. We plan for things to be taken care of while we are away like the mail, the house or pets. We may need passports or new luggage so we run around and prepare for a wonderful vacation. Once the date comes and we get in the car or step on that plane or ship, it is time to release all the planning and preparation and enjoy our vacation!

I recently received a phone call from a woman who was looking for a publisher for a book she had written. She asked if I could give her some advice. I inquired about her book proposal and if she had prepared a query letter. I also asked if she had researched editors who specialized in her particular genre. She became agitated and stated that she did not intend to do any of those things and that her book was so good that any publisher would be excited to work with her. I tried to explain that she needed to do her homework first and if she wanted a mainstream publisher, she would have to complete a book proposal. Most publishers would not accept a completed manuscript and many will only work through an agent. With that, she became furious and her voice rose as she stated that her book was so good she was fearful an agent or editor might steal it. It was hidden where no one would ever find it.

Barbara Miller

Wow! This is a classic example of working against yourself. Talk about anxiety. She was actually sabotaging any possibilities of ever getting her book published out of fear of releasing it to a publisher. She was so paranoid of what might happen that she wasn't allowing herself to take the necessary steps to reach her goal. I suggested she self-publish her book to keep more control and that suggestion made her even more upset. It was like saying, "I have a great invention that will benefit the world, but I am afraid someone will steal my idea so I have it hidden in a safe place." Yes, this is ridiculous, but the reality of your life is what is happening right now, at this very moment. Tomorrow or next week is merely speculation. This moment is all you can be certain of. It is almost impossible for our creative genius to work when we allow so much stress by thinking and worrying about everything. Appropriate planning and then releasing will free our creative genius to do its part. It will serve you well to relax and let go.

Several years ago, just before I opened my day spa, my daughter walked in my office and asks, "Mother, why do you have pictures of that smiling guru, 'Sorry, Tony' and that dead man on your desk?" The dead man was Napoleon Hill. I sheepishly said, "They are my advisors and you just interrupted a very important meeting." With that, the infamous right eyebrow lifted, as only Alison can do. She gave me that you're joking right look and said, "Mother, please do not tell anyone that you hold meetings with Tony Robbins and Napoleon Hill or everyone will know you have gone completely loopy!"

Then her curiosity got the best of her. She sat down and asked, "What can two photos do for you, Mother?" I said, "Well, I meditate on what I want from life and then call on my *Master*

60

Minds, as Napoleon Hill calls them, to help me get it." Up went the eyebrow again. "Mother, how can looking at photos accomplish this?" I explained that we are made up of energy and vibrations. The entire universe vibrates to a rhythm and when we connect with the *Universal Mind* and enter the same frequency as other like minds, we can make our requests known and just simply expect results. She said, "That sounds way too simple, Mother. Just because I want or need something and tell the Universe, does not mean I am going to get it." Well, it depends on why you want it and what your motives are for acquiring it. The universe has nothing but abundance and we are intricately connected to that universe.

I had always wanted to attend a Tony Robbins' seminar and participate in his infamous *Fire Walk.* I received a flyer in the mail one day announcing that Tony Robbins was offering his Unleash the Power seminar in Chicago and only the brave and the bold would participate in the *Fire Walk* that weekend. I was ecstatic as I could drive from Grand Rapids to Chicago in three hours. I immediately picked up the phone and made my reservation.

I stayed at a nearby hotel and drove to the seminar location. As I walked into the meeting room, I was astounded by the number of people already seated. I felt very conspicuous as I grabbed the nearest seat. The meeting started with a crescendo and a mass of moving energy, the likes I had never known, and intensified for the entire three days! My first thoughts were 'Lord help me, I have just walked into the *twilight zone!*' The second Tony Robbins walked on that stage, the crowd began cheering and applauding with such intensity that it felt like the entire room might explode!

Barbara Miller

We were forced to interact with the people sitting next to us and I was lucky to be sitting beside a mother and her two sons. Paula had been to a previous Tony Robbins' seminar and had promised to take her two sons as soon as another seminar came to Chicago. So here we all were full of excitement and expectation as we listened for gems of enlightenment that we might take away with us. It was a surprise to learn that Paula and her sons were staying at the same hotel as me. We connected immediately and she invited me to ride to the meetings with the three of them.

The entire experience turned out to be one of the most empowering weekends of my entire life. It was like a dark corner of my brain lit up for the first time and all I wanted to do was learn more. I hung onto every word and never stopped taking notes. I learned about the magic of dreaming big and focusing on what I really wanted in life and then setting goals for myself. Things that I had felt were impossible for me to achieve, seemed possible and believable. I had never been taught that I could do anything I set my mind to. I sat looking at this famous guru who was telling me anything was possible and not only that but he was believable!

The only problem with the weekend was it wasn't long enough. It flew by and there we were on our last night, sitting in the audience listening to this crazy big guy telling us we could walk on fire heated to 2000 degrees. The crowd was pulsating with an energy that had a life of its own; often reaching such crescendos that I thought the roof would literally blow off the building. You not only could feel the energy but you became part of the energy! I had never witnessed anything quite like this in my life. Tony had everyone all psyched up into a lather and ready to embrace the moment, jumping up and down, dancing in the aisles and convinced that they could walk on fire. Yes, real hot burning coals of fire! The ridiculous thing was that I believed it too.

So, when the time came, we all marched outside chanting, shouting and screaming, "Yes I can, yes I can!" There was no time to be afraid. When it was my turn, Paula was right behind me shouting, "You can do it, Barbara! Yes, yes, yes!" I was told not to look down, just walk straight ahead. I felt like I was in a trance state, almost like being spiritually separated from my body. I did not even know I was at the end of the Fire Walk until people were grabbing me and yelling "Yes, yes, you did it. You did the Fire Walk!" I DID IT! I could not believe that I had in fact just walked on red hot coals. It was the most *outrageous* thing I had ever done! How did that happen and I did not feel the heat? We were all totally committed to doing the Fire Walk. Tony taught us to overcome limiting beliefs, like my instincts saying, 'Are you nuts, girl? Run!' However, my mind was primed and ready to walk fearlessly. Tony just simply expected every one of us to walk those hot embers. I went from a state of fear to one of power. Johann Wolfgang von Goethe says, *"Whatever you can do or dream you can, begin it. Boldness has genius, power, and magic in it."*

Tony Robbins teaches that to overcome our fears we must use anchoring effectively. I had no idea what anchoring meant. I learned that it is simply reliving an event or time in your life when you felt empowered by an accomplishment you were applauded for achieving. Perhaps you could recall a time when you received an award or met a challenge by stepping out of your comfort zone. Tony says just recall those moments and it will change your state from one of doubt and fear to one of success and confidence. He teaches that the only limitations we experience are self-imposed. When we get past this fear by using anchoring, we become unstoppable! All we have to do is take the first step and we can master whatever we set our mind to, even the infamous Fire Walk! Yes, you can!

Brenda's Story

I was so excited to marry Justin. He was so handsome and intelligent. I had just graduated high school and even though I had always dreamed of going to college, I felt it was impossible. I came from a poor family and my father made it very clear that I would get no assistance from him and that I should just get a job and take care of myself. My home life was a daily struggle with constant arguing and sometimes physical outbursts from my father. Marrying Justin was a way to escape to a better life.

Justin was 15 years older and had an executive position in a large corporation. We enjoyed the finer things in life and for a few years everything seemed okay. I did not like the way Justin controlled everything, and constantly preached how he was older, wiser, and a good provider. He would not allow me to work and insisted that he made more than enough money and he expected me to stay home.

I was very disappointed over the years that I was unable to have children. The doctor could not find any apparent reason for my infertility, but my husband insisted that it was my problem and there was nothing wrong with him. We discussed adoption but he would always ignore my requests to contact adoption agencies. I finally gave up and devoted my time to volunteer work and interior design. I had helped several friends decorate their homes and shop for the right furniture and accessories. This was my love and kept me somewhat fulfilled.

I suspected that Justin had started having affairs and even though he vehemently denied it, I still had a nagging suspicion that I was right. He was returning home later in the evenings and often missing dinner. When I would question where he had been, he became verbally abusive and sometimes stormed out and returned smelling of alcohol.

I was finally shaken out of my complacency when my husband announced that he had found someone else and wanted a divorce. The shock of hearing it confirmed by him left me paralyzed with fear. He wanted to share an attorney to keep the cost of the divorce down. He kept insisting that he should get more in a settlement as he had been the sole bread winner for 10 years and I had contributed nothing.

I had a close friend who had gone through a harrowing divorce and I immediately called her and sobbed through telling her what had happened. She was kind and sympathetic but adamant that I get my own attorney at once. She also insisted that I have an attorney put a hold on all accounts to keep him from hiding assets. I was so scared I could hardly breathe. I had never stood up to him before and I was not certain of how he might react. My friend insisted I call her female attorney, who specialized in helping women get their fair share in divorce settlements. Although terrified, I called and made an appointment.

I met with the attorney and tearfully signed the divorce papers. I instructed her to serve him at work as I was afraid of his reaction. As I suspected, he was furious! He screamed and yelled at me on the phone, shouting obscenities and threats, but I stood my ground and said "You wanted a divorce and you are getting what you asked for."

It was a long and drawn-out battle, and I am certain he hid much of the money, but it was finally over. I did get to keep the house, which he had insisted on selling. I was not certain how long I would keep my home but at least it was my decision to make. Now I had to decide what to do with my life, which was also my decision to make. Friends encouraged me to enroll in an interior design school and pursue what I loved. I had already been thinking about this option and their support gave me the encouragement I needed to move forward with my life.

It was about six months after my divorce before I enrolled in school, but it has been a wonderful healing catalyst. Friends have already been networking for me to help get me started in my new career. I feel more excitement than I have experienced in my entire life. I did not realize that I was going through a numb programmed existence until I was finally set free. Justin has already remarried and she is 20 years younger and pregnant. I don't feel hateful towards them, I just feel sad, but I am determined to keep focused on my goal to start my new life.

No matter how carefully we plan our life; there will always be changes that interrupt the best laid plans. The key is to not let the unexpected derail you and your plans; just readjust and continue. I did not welcome or want the changes divorce brought to my life but it wasn't until I accepted the change as a fact that I was able to move forward. The point is we can all lose our power to change by denial, anger, or bitterness; or we can choose to face what life has dealt us.

I tell in my book, *You Lost Your Marriage Not Your Life*, how I refused to hire a lawyer because I would have to admit that my husband was never coming back and my marriage was over. Consequently, he had several months to hide money and assets. Once I faced the fact that divorce was still happening no matter how hard I fought against it, only then could I begin to see clearly and act rationally to bring balance and control back to my life.

- What changes are you resisting in your life?
- Is there something you need to face or accept?
- Are you carrying seeds of bitterness that need to be released before they take root and grow?
- Are you still trying to control everything and everybody?

"Inaction breeds doubt and fear. Action breeds confidence and courage. If you want to conquer fear, do not sit home and think about it. Go out and get busy." Dale Carnegie.

Have you taken time to reflect on what you want for your own life and where you want to go? Whatever you decide, make certain that you are not coming from a place of desperation. Are you doing what you love or are you dancing to someone else's plans for your life? Perhaps you were programmed from youth that you must follow in a parent's footsteps and take over the family business. You know down deep that you hate working under their thumb but are too afraid to speak up. They might not even realize that you have goals and dreams of your own. Maybe it is time to stand up, speak out and make your desires known. No one else can decide your future unless you let them.

If you cannot hear the sound of the genuine in you, you will all of your life spend your days on the ends of strings that somebody else pull. Howard Thurman

Chapter 5
DANCE OF WORDS

"The language you use is very powerful. It alters your perception and confirms your expectations. How you feel about yourself, others, and life is greatly influenced by the language that you use in that almost nonstop conversation that's going on in your head." Alan Gettis, Ph.D.

Watch your thoughts—listen to them because they shape your life and evolve into words. They tell a story about you and how you perceive your life. What are you thinking about? What is your inner voice telling you? Are your thoughts positive and uplifting or negative and condemning? Do you always feel compelled to find fault with everything and everyone? Do you think people are judging you or rejecting you? Then change your thoughts! The only one limiting you is you!

Always see yourself in the setting you want—sharing with friends and for once not wondering what *they think* about you, daring to imagine a new love in your life or that *dream job*. Whatever you want, just see yourself accomplishing it. I imagined myself standing at a podium in front of a large audience. They were smiling and applauding with anticipation for my speech. I saw myself sitting at a table with my books stacked up and people lined up waiting to purchase my autographed books.

Don't be thinking about how you are going to make things happen or the process; just see yourself experiencing your goals or dreams. Really feel it, get excited, emotional, breathe it and it will come to fruition, and as I mentioned earlier, leave the details to the Universe; it knows what to do. Your thoughts send out vibrations into the Universe, seeking and connecting to whomever or whatever needs to happen to bring your thoughts to things. Dare to be happy and live in anticipation as you focus on your wonderful future.

Step out of the past. Start living in the present and looking forward to the future. Even though our past bears record of how we got where we are now, it certainly does not have to determine where our present and future take us. We cannot change any of the circumstances that occurred in our past, but stepping out of our past and setting our feet firmly in the present is the first move toward wholeness. The only way we can do anything to create a fulfilling future is to focus on what is happening right now.

Kathryn's Story

My husband and I could not have been more thrilled with our life. We had entered into a business venture with a man from our church. We were so convinced that this was an answer to prayer that we would be part of a new company offering accounting services to local businesses. My husband was an accountant and had created a new company with a CPA. We did not hesitate when our new partner asked us to put up our share of the startup costs. Even though it was all the money we had, my husband was so excited that I felt confident all would be well.

While we were living on next to nothing, we couldn't help but notice that he sported a brand-new red sports car and his wife came to church showing off her new fur jacket. As the weeks went by and no substantial business was coming in, we began to feel a sense of panic. We had turned over our entire life's savings and could barely get by each day. We started hearing rumors at church about the company our business partner had kept books for and handled their money were questioning some discrepancies in his accounting. We heard that he was being accused of embezzling thousands of dollars over the years and they were going to press charges.

While we were desperately trying to make sense of everything, the bitter realization began to take hold. We had turned over our retirement money to a con artist from our own church. We tried to talk to him, but he was not returning any calls. In desperation, we went to our pastor and were told that this was an area beyond his scope and we should consult an attorney. We made an appointment with our attorney but before our scheduled meeting took place, we got the shocking news. Our business partner had killed himself. At first, we were overwhelmed with shock, but after the shock wore off, we had to face this terrible loss. Not only were we now penniless but we had been deceived by a man we trusted in our own church!

Much to our amazement, the church elders absolved themselves of any involvement and refused to discuss anything regarding this issue. We thought they would at least give us support and sympathy, but we were totally rejected. Not only were we rejected, but from the pulpit our pastor shared his sadness over the death of this man, and then had the audacity to ask the entire congregation to, "Just let this go and do not attempt to find out any details out of respect for his family." Of course, there was no mention of prayers for my husband and me and all that we had lost.

We were forced into bankruptcy and lost everything we had because we had trusted the wrong man. He had been a pillar in the church for twenty years. I keep trying to let go of the past, but the anger and bitterness I feel at his wicked deception has nearly destroyed me. I don't want to keep digging up the past and opening up old wounds, but I cannot let it go and it haunts me daily. How can I ever forgive a dead man for ruining our lives and then taking it to the grave? I wish I could dig him up and kill him all over again!"

I don't know what precautions Kathryn and her husband took before handing over all their money. Apparently, there were no checks and balances in place to help safeguard their investment, and in reality, they could have done everything right and still been taken advantage of. This is a tragic story of trust, deceit and betrayal, but whether their lives were ruined or not was strictly up to Kathryn and her husband. Constantly reminding yourself of something someone did or said that hurt you cannot change the act itself. Retaliating against people who have hurt and mistreated you will simply keep the pain alive until it eats away at your soul. Perhaps if their business partner had not killed himself, Kathryn and her husband might have been able to bring him to justice in a court of law. This might have helped with their feelings of helplessness and anger. As it was, they were left in complete shock and could not get over the betrayal of their trust by a church elder.

I always looked to outside experiences or people to make me happy or tell me what to do. I could not perceive that I was the one who controlled my own happiness. I looked to relationships to find happiness and when those relationships failed, I felt hurt, rejected and isolated, not realizing the key to my own happiness was within me. I was unknowingly setting myself up for rejection by expecting others to fill my aching void. Having come from a background of dysfunction and violence, I carried with me the thoughts that something bad was going to happen so I unwittingly set the stage in all my relationships for something "bad" to happen.

When my daughter Alison was three years old, she came to me and said, "Mommy, I'm scared." I asked her why she felt scared and this is what she said. "*I'm scared because everyone is cardboard and I am the only one who is real, and you are cardboard and I am afraid that you will disappear and I will be left all alone.*" What was my precious little girl picking up on

Barbara Miller

with the people nearest and dearest to her? I really think it was my quelled spirit. I was going through terrible depression in those days. I harbored buried pain from my earlier life and struggled with not knowing how to deal with it. The key to finally looking at my pain was a miracle. I was having lunch with a friend one day and I was sharing with her about how depressed I was and I had been seeing a psychologist. I was having nightmares and they were terrifying. The nightmares were now constant and nearly every night I awakened screaming. She studied me and said, "I think the problem, Barbara, is that you need God in your life and I would like to take you to my Bible study class." I agreed to go even though I was convinced that nothing could help me. However, my daughter's words kept ringing in my ears. "I am scared because you are cardboard."

I began attending regular Bible study and Alison was in the children's program. The leader was a wonderful woman named Char and the role she played in my healing was immeasurable. At first, I was very quiet, just listening and keeping everyone at a distance but as time went on and I began to grasp the message of healing and forgiveness, my life began to change. I began to see how much anger I was suppressing and just how deep I had buried my childhood pain. My anger would surface without warning, like the time I had been standing in line waiting to get the following week's lesson. When two women came up and got in front of me, I stepped out of line, reached in front of them and grabbed the paper from a very shocked woman, stating, "I have been standing here, waiting." I was so embarrassed at my behavior that I shared it on the phone with Char. She said, "Barbara, I was thinking today that I would like to introduce you to my friend Hugh. He is a lay spiritual counselor and I think he might be able to help you work through some of your problems." I did not know whether to be angry or happy but I agreed to go.

This was all foreign to me and I was not so sure about what I was getting myself into, especially since he was a lay counselor and did not even charge for his services. However, once I met this gentle, non-judgmental, spiritual man, I felt instantly at ease. Over the course of the next two years, Hugh worked with me, teaching me spiritual truths about what God says about me. He called it Spiritual Therapy. I discovered that my past does not have to define who I am today. I do not have to struggle and berate myself for past mistakes because God sees me as a perfect human being. I learned that looking to others to validate me would only bring more pain. I was already validated by the Creator of the Universe and he created everything perfect and good. I did not have to strive to attempt to be perfect; all I had to do was rest in the fact that God loves and accepts me just as I am. I learned that God doesn't make mistakes and many of the past abuses I had suffered would one day hold great value because I would be able to help others who have also suffered. Hugh explained that I had no control over choosing my parents but I did have control over those I chose to share my current life with.

It wasn't until I finally learned what it meant to take charge of self-defeating thoughts that change began to come to my life. My thoughts controlled me by constantly reminded me that I'm not good enough, I'm not smart enough, they don't like me, why would anyone want me as a friend? Hugh helped me realize that the truest thing about me was what God said, not what my negative thoughts tried to tell me was true. I was eventually able to check those thoughts at once and replace them with positive ones. We live most of our time in our thoughts and what we focus on determines our life. It is crucial that we recognize this truth and become acutely aware of any negative or self-deprecating thoughts. They must immediately be stopped short and banished; then replaced with positive uplifting thoughts.

Alison and I stayed in the Bible study class for three years. During that first year, while we were out running errands, I heard the most profound singing coming from the back seat of the car. My beautiful little daughter was singing praises from the book of Psalms. The children in the Bible study always had lessons from the same books of the Bible as the mothers. Of course, theirs was prepared for children. I said, "Wow, honey, your singing sounds like angels." She said, "I am so happy and I'm not scared, Mommy, because you are not cardboard anymore. You are *real!*" Tears began pouring down my face and to this day I will never fully understand how this little child could look inside and view my soul and know if I was real. What a deep mystery!

I was finally able to recognize the pain I had shoved down deep for so many years and look at it for what it was; it was the thief of my joy. My pain was not willing to leave instantly; it had been my constant companion for many years and it liked my company. Over the years, I had managed to put on a convincing façade. I looked happy and put together and belonged to women's clubs and volunteered for different charities. I modeled for exclusive shops and department stores but underneath this seemingly strong woman was a deep longing to be *real*. It took a tiny child to help point the way.

Have you ever been around an obviously unhappy person? I don't mean someone who has suffered a loss, I mean a perpetually unhappy person. Every time you ask them, "How are you doing?" you always get the same answer, "Oh, I'm okay" then they look down and mope and look like they have the weight of the world on their shoulders. They have a unique way of making you feel responsible for how they feel. Or you ask, "How is your day going?" and you get, "Oh, it could be better." And then they proceed to give you a detailed accounting as to why their life isn't going well. Continuing on this path will only bring more of the same, unhappiness. It is not my or your responsibility to cheer people up or make them happy. It is not in our job description! Some people are comfortable in their depressed blue funk and really do not want to change, especially if they can find a sympathetic listener. Do not let their negative influence drag you down.

Complainers get their daily fix by doing what they do best—complaining! In the meantime, they wonder why people begin avoiding them and stop returning their calls. They are in a vicious cycle as they complain and brood about *'poor me.'* They are enveloped in their own self-destructive need to always find fault and they have shrunk-wrapped themselves into a tight, self-centered life of conflict. They spend their lives in conflict with family, conflict at work and even at play. They create their own misery. Have you ever been accosted by their issues, feel exhausted even though you have held captive by their chatter and not given a chance to utter a word, only to have them say, "Oh thank you, I just needed someone to talk to?" What they really meant was someone to—talk at! If you wake up each day and think with a critical spirit, unhappiness will greet you and be your companion for as long as *you* allow it!

This does not mean that when our friends or a family member is suffering that we should ignore them; it simply means that for many people, it is a pattern they have embraced for so long that it now engulfs their entire life. They spend their life focusing on themselves and how rotten and difficult life is and why everybody else gets all the breaks, and desperately need an ear—any ear that will listen to their tales of woe. If you see yourself described here, maybe it is time to take a look at where all this negative verbiage came from. Maybe you are just in a cycle of reruns from what you learned as a child from your mother or father. What compels this need in you to complain and how can you change this behavior to a more positive note?

Sitting around and conversing with negative people will take its toll on your psychological wellbeing. Of course, it is okay if you have a depressing situation in your life and need to talk it through with a friend or family member, but I am talking about regular routine chronic complaining. All of those negative thoughts and words go out into the Universe, breeding more dark thoughts. If this is a habit you have allowed to run your life, it is time to take charge and start focusing on all the wonderful opportunities available to you.

If you do not check your negative thoughts and words, they will begin to affect your health. Depression is a common problem and most of us have experienced depression at some point in our lives, but if it is allowed to continue it can cause physical problems and literally make you sick! You must take control and decide for yourself to put up a mental "stop sign" to your mind. Whenever you find yourself allowing negative, disparaging thoughts to run rampant like a freeway with no speed limit, just put up your "stop" sign. Think of the healing white light of the Universe and rest in God's love and peace.

I had never considered that my negative thoughts and attitudes could actually infect others like a virus. Joel Osteen in his book, *Your Best Life Now: 7 Steps to Living at Your Full Potential*, warns us, "*If you must be around a pessimist, be sure to guard against their negative attitudes infecting your thinking*." Wow, that's a terrifying thought and I surely do not want to give someone a "negative infection."

We simply must agree to stop our pessimistic attitudes and fill our minds with positive thoughts of gratitude and thanksgiving to the God of the Universe for all of life's blessings. If you want a life of peace and joy, remember your thoughts manifest from the inside to the outside. Check your thoughts and if they are all critical and negative, take inventory of how they directly correlate with your life! Think on good things and good things will appear. Think on bad things and they will appear as well. Which would you prefer? Is it really fun having a gloom and doom party? If you sent out invitations, how many people would want to come?

Even though our past bears record of how we got to where we are now, it certainly does not have to determine where our present and future take us. Stepping out of our past and setting our feet firmly in the present is the first step toward wholeness. As the words to an old Mama Cass song go, "Make your own kind of music." Her lyrics tell us that we each have our own *special song*. Remember the old movie, Casablanca, where

Barbara Miller

Ingrid Bergman says, "Play it again, Sam"? I think it is time we break that old record and make our own *"special song."* Are you singing your own *special song* or are you hardwired to keep playing the same old painful song of your past? Now is the time to give space to a new song.

The current economy has gotten a lot of people in a depressed mode and rightly so in many ways. It is no fun to lose our money, our home, job security and, for many, their marriages, but looking to your Higher Power to help redirect your life and see you through times of trouble will give you a sense of peace instead of panic. The Living Bible tells us, *"So don't be anxious about tomorrow. God will take care of your tomorrow too. Live one day at a time."*

Many years ago, at the age of twenty-one, I was the first woman ever hired in a certain real estate office. This was a valuable learning experience that benefited me for most of my adult life. Between my quick tongue and critical nature, I had a lot to learn. I had wonderful training by many of the men in my office who thought it was their responsibility to teach this young chick the ropes. They reluctantly allowed me to go along on their appointments with the understanding that I was to keep my mouth shut and just listen. I thought this was rather harsh but I wanted to learn so I agreed.

There was no such thing in those days as real estate school. The weeks I spent tagging along on property showings and listing and sales presentations was the foundation of teaching me the dance of dealing with emotions, and the step, twirl, curtsy that are all woven into direct sales. I learned that people buy and sell emotionally. Sometimes their reasons make absolutely no sense to anyone else, but if you try to argue with them or push them into what you think they should do, you will suddenly find yourself with tread marks across your feet as they speed off to find another realtor!

You have heard the expression: I don't take any crap from anybody. Well, guess what? You will if you live long enough. This is a wild and crazy planet we live on and there are plenty of people to get in your face on a daily basis. If we want to escape being victims of road rage or being lashed out at by angry people we come in contact with, we will then understand the importance of learning the *Dance of Words*. When we lose control of our emotions or temper, we lose! Is it okay to confront? Of course, it is, if appropriate. Being walked on, insulted, abused are all reasons to confront, as long as your goal is not just to tell someone off. Yelling, screaming, demanding and threatening is a no-win situation and you have now put yourself on their level. Take "the road less traveled" and walk away.

When I want to confront a friend or family member, I have found what works best for me is a well thought out letter. I don't mean just venting on paper instead of verbally. My first concern is that my letter be written in a spirit of love. I ask the Universe to bless my letter that the words and meaning be received in the spirit I have intended. In writing a letter, it forces me to put my own opinion and feelings down in front of me. I then have the opportunity to read it over the next day and ask myself: *Is this really what I wanted to say and is it worth it?* The majority of times I shred the letter and let it go. I learned the hard way that any time you enter into a battle of words with a loved one or an acquaintance, you lose the battle once the words have hit their heart like an arrow. You have stirred them into shooting back. Choose your words or learn to keep silent! Don't search for a role model—be one.

In writing a letter to a combative person, you have an opportunity to express your concerns without interruption or anger that can erupt into a full-blown argument. Don't go there. Nothing is worth a shouting match with someone you love. You risk, as I have done in the past, saying hurtful things you cannot take back. Many times, it is important to confront if a friend or family member has deeply hurt you. They need to know that just because you love them; it is not a license for verbal abuse. My mother used to tell us when we were living at home that just because you did not get your way or were not feeling well did not give you a license to be mean.

In his book, *It's All Part of the Dance: Finding Happiness in an Upside Down World*, Alan Gettis, Ph.D. says, "*We could just as easily say that happiness is found between stimulus and response.*" In other words, take a time-out before you shoot those arrows and give space to your words. Maybe you remember the old saying our parents quoted when other kids were being mean. 'Sticks and stones can break my bones, but word can never hurt me.' What a lie! Words can in fact kill a soul. All you have to do is listen to the news on the results of one person bullying another to the point they commit suicide.

I was once part of a care-share group from my church and we each took turns leading our small group on different topics. I was the designated leader for our next meeting and the topic was, "Is it okay to have conflict with fellow church members or friends and not have to apologize if you were unjustly critical or insulting?" There was a particular woman who tended to dominate the conversation at each gathering. She was quick to offer her opinion. It was her belief that because she was a Christian, and insulted another Christian, it was okay to let it go and not apologize. They should automatically know that we are already forgiven for our mistakes. I sat there stunned. Total silence filled the room and all eyes were on me, with the exception of her husband, who just looked down and appeared very embarrassed. It was clear that he had been at the receiving end of her insults and obviously carried wounds.

I sent up a *help me* plea to the Universe and then carefully stated my opinion. I said, "I personally feel that when we have deliberately or inadvertently hurt someone, no matter who it is, a quick apology works miracles. You could say, "I am so sorry. That was a thoughtless remark, please forgive me." When you ask forgiveness, it goes a long way toward healing harsh words. I think as God's representatives we have an even greater responsibility to be caring and loving. This does not mean that we can never disagree or challenge someone on a subject, but our choice of words will always determine the outcome. I feel that if we never take responsibility for our words, we may wake up one morning and have no one to insult because those we proclaim to love have all abandoned us."

She looked thoughtful and then said quietly, "I never even considered that before. I should really guard my words more closely and follow the old rule, *think before you speak*. Thank you, Barbara, for making me aware of the impact my criticisms may have had. I will have to make a list of those I may owe an apology to."

We are not always going to say the right thing or choose the right words, but understanding how our words impact others is crucial to our own wellbeing and happiness. Being slow to speak and offer an opinion will make you a wise steward in mastering the *dance of words*. When our words are out there, they are forever out there, reverberating through time and space, and not a single fishing rod in the entire world can reel them back in. Choosing the right time to speak and when to remain silent will serve you well as you step into your best life yet!

It is not always what people say, but how we react to it that can impact our lives. When we react to criticism and retaliate in kind, we become powerless. Nothing makes us more vulnerable than being out of control. Even a hot temper can be kept in check if we are really in tune to why we over react to other's comments or insults.

Michelle's Story

My husband was so difficult to live with and was the master of snide remarks and sarcasm. We could not even enjoy a dinner out without him criticizing someone walking by or sitting at a nearby table. He would make comments like, "That woman is chewing with her mouth open and I cannot stand watching her." My response was,
"Well, quit looking at her." He was staring at a couple so blatantly one evening while dining out that I asked them if my husband could join them. Of course, he was livid at my comment and dinner was ruined.

He constantly found fault with me and corrected my English routinely. He said, "I do not want you to embarrass yourself so I feel it is necessary so people will respect you." I put up with his hurtful tactics for many years until he began criticizing our daughter. We were getting ready for church one Sunday morning when our daughter walked into the kitchen. She was nine years old. He studied her and said, "You are not really planning on wearing that to church, are you? I want everyone to be proud of my daughter." The look on my poor child's face was so painful, I determined right then that I had had enough of his verbal insults. I said, "She looks beautiful and there is nothing wrong with her choice of what she should wear to church." She started to cry and went back to her room to change. He had hurt her so deeply. She was always a sensitive soul and so gentle. I was determined not to allow him to break her spirit or destroy her self-confidence like he had mine.

When she left the room, I confronted him, saying, "Don't you ever insult my child again. There are gentle loving ways to correct or guide and your sarcasm has gone on way too long. She is a sensitive soul and you have hurt her deeply." He looked startled and retaliated by not speaking to either one of us, but I didn't care. I had finally stood up to him.

We were at a party at a friend's house and were chatting and mingling when an older gentleman commented to my husband about me. He said, "Your wife is so beautiful and outgoing, I bet she is a wonderful wife." I was totally shocked when he replied, "Well, she is a good mother." I was so humiliated and embarrassed. I felt betrayed and diminished and the man was taken so far off guard, he just backed up and turned and walked away.

Barbara Miller

I felt like I lived in a no-win situation and wondered why this man that I had loved would constantly want to put me down. I felt powerless and insecure as a woman and when our daughter was in high school, I finally divorced him. I could not take his incessant belittling any longer. He died a few years later, a miserable, lonely, bitter man.

I tried so desperately to change him and make him happy. I finally realized that I could not possibly change him. He was the only person who could invite change into his life. Now I feel content to finally find peace and joy as I work to build a new future. I had such low self-esteem from all those years of verbal abuse that I had to seek counseling. Counseling helped me understand that I did nothing wrong and I no longer had to play the role of victim. I learned that we are not responsible for the happiness of another person, but we can be responsible for making another miserable.

Criticism, fault finding, and the need to control can certainly cause our spouse to lose respect for us and withdraw their love, which is what Michelle did as a result of years of condescending behavior from her husband.

"Think twice before you speak, because your words and influence will plant the seed of either success or failure in the mind of another." Napoleon Hill

How can we protect ourselves from falling into a life of disrespect and misery? It must begin with you. If you have been programmed from childhood, as I was, to believe you have to live with this behavior, I am here to tell you otherwise. You have within you the ability and fortitude to stand up and be strong. If the messages and signals you send out are "I am vulnerable and insecure so go ahead and abuse and belittle me" then that is exactly what you will attract. Replacing those old belief patterns with positive thoughts and inner healing will put out new vibrations into the Universe that say, "Don't even try it, buster. *I am beautiful, I am strong, and I am a princess!"*

It is a painful process to allow past hurts and abuses to rise to the surface and be exposed to the light. However, in order to find strength and healing, it is the only way. Living a life of defeat and sadness is no life for a princess!

My friend Marilyn emailed me this story a few years ago and I do not know the author, but I gave it a new twist and like to call it the *true story* of The Princess and the Frog.

Once upon a time a beautiful princess was out in her lovely garden doing her morning meditations and writing in her Positive Thoughts Journal. Suddenly, without warning, a large slimy green frog jumped in the middle of her book and, much to her amazement the creature began to speak. "Please, my beautiful lady. I was formerly a handsome prince until a wicked witch cast a spell on me and reduced me to this lowly creature forced to dine on flies and bugs just to sustain myself. My mother the queen was cast out of the kingdom and forced to live as a commoner. If I could receive one kiss, just one kiss, from a true princess, it will break the spell of the wicked witch and turn me back into a handsome prince.

You can take me to your castle and we will marry and you can bear my children and cook, clean, and sew beautiful clothing for us, and Mom can come and live with us and be restored to Queen. You can take care of running the castle and caring for our beautiful children while Mom and I run your kingdom. Then in the evenings, I will retire to the drawing room to relax while you feed the children, clean up the kitchen, give the children their baths, tuck them in bed, read bedtime stories, oh, and serve Mom her evening tea. Then join me in the drawing room and we will reflect on our wonderful life together."

The princess quickly slammed her book shut, laughing hysterically! "Silly frog." Later that evening, as candlelight danced on the castle walls, the princess sat reviewing her online commerce site, posting to the Princess Diary Blog, and admiring her new frog mouse pad. You could hear her exclaim, "Flies, bugs, Mom, and a green frog living in my castle? Ha, ha, ha, ha! That just doesn't work for me!"

You do not need a man to make you happy and you certainly don't need to kiss a frog. Only you can make you happy. The man you love can add new dimension to your happiness, but happiness is a choice you must make for yourself. Perhaps you always doubt your significant other's love and feel like you must work at getting his attention. These may be early warning signs that you are not the top priority in his life. You deserve to feel secure in your relationship and know that you are the most important woman in the world to him—like a *princess.*

I love what Dr. Phil stated in one of his episodes on the Doctor Phil Show. He was challenging a male guest for demeaning his wife. He pointed to his own wife Robin, who always sits in the audience and said, "There is not a single day that goes by that I don't wake up and ask what I could do to make it a better day for that woman." Now that is a *princely* attitude fit for a *princess!* Chances are if you don't feel it, it isn't there, and all the pleading and whining will not create a love that does not exist. Follow your instincts!

Emotional stability is a must in any relationship. Observe how he treats his friends. Does he have friends or is he a loner? What are his relationships like with his family; and if he has grown children, what are the relationships like? Is he estranged from his family? Watch how he interacts with his parents, especially his mother, as this may reflect how he treats you. Although I do believe there are circumstances that justify a man or a woman severing relationships with certain family members, hopefully he will tell you at some point what those reasons are. Men respond differently to different women, but if he is emotionally unstable, those old patterns will eventually surface as he begins to let his guard down. Remember, you cannot fix him; it is up to him to recognize the need to change. If he is not willing to even discuss his issues, ask yourself: *Is this what I want for the rest of my life?* If the answer is no, hit the road!

- Do you consider the words you choose and their impact on others?
- Are you suffering verbal abuse in your life at the hands of a love one?
- What changes do you need to make to set ground rules for respect?
- Are you being treated respectfully by your spouse of significant other?

"Your time is limited, don't waste it living someone else's life. Don't be trapped by dogma, which is living

the result of other people's thinking. Don't let the voice of other's opinion drown your own inner voice. And most important, have the courage to follow your heart and intuition, they somehow already know what you truly want to become. Everything else is secondary."
Steve Jobs

Chapter 6
DANCE OF HAPPINESS

Pick the day. Enjoy it—to the hilt. The day as it comes.
People as they come. The past I think has helped me
appreciate the present—and I don't want to spoil any
of it by fretting about the future. Audrey Hepburn,
actress

Embrace happiness as part of who you are now, not some marks of achievement you have set for your future. Happiness should not be a condition of when you have accomplished your goals, found the right job, moved into the right neighborhood, or met the right man. Happiness is a *now* choice! If you are looking for outside circumstances to create your happiness then you look in vain. There will never be a perfect event to bring happiness. You may have temporary joy or excitement, but true happiness must be cultivated or practiced as a way of life. Resist the attitude that you will be happy when.... Decide to be happy now!

to go only so far? Does someone else determine our happiness? Where does happiness reside and how can we find this elusive place? We all have particular highs in our life like falling in love, winning a competition or special recognition. We feel overjoyed with our expectant pregnancy, new home, car, friends; but this elevated joy is not happiness. We have all met those contented, optimistic souls who wear a perpetual smile and always appear so positive and stable. They seem to always be happy for no reason.

Tal Ben-Shahar, PhD, a Harvard University lecturer says being born with the right combination of genes might determine the happiness set point, but there are steps one can take to increase the level of happiness. Being social and connected in the world is a major player in happiness. Even though our genes can impact our happiness level, there are still steps we can take to become happier. He emphasizes that what we choose to focus on, as opposed to what we have or our social status in life, will have an effect on our happiness. If you are constantly looking to outside stimulus, monetary gain or possessions as a means to find happiness, you will be sorely disappointed.

Some believe that wealth will bring them the happiness they seek; however, studies on lottery winners are a perfect example. There may be a time of elation with their new found wealth, but most go through the money and end up exactly where they were before and not a bit happier.

Is happiness all in your head? Well, yes, actually it is. Happy marriages, friendships, close family ties, acquaintances, fulfilling work are all factors in how happy you will be. A positive outlook on life and strong values seems natural ingredients for those who are connected. Also, learning something new is a great stimulator for happiness genes. The brain thrives on meeting new challenges; even if you volunteer in a hospital, your brain loves it. According to Tel Ben-Shahar, to be truly happy we must be fully engaged in our day to day living and not be constantly anticipating a lottery win or a job promotion to provide happiness.

Have you ever watched children living in deplorable conditions? They play and run around, laughing and chasing one another. They are happy in the moment despite their surroundings. The point is we can find many reasons *not* to be happy. The nitty-gritty everyday problems and burdens will often leave us down and discouraged, but choosing and practicing a happy attitude will bring peace even in turmoil. It is not the circumstances or disappointments in life that cause our unhappiness. It is our reaction to them.

Do not depend on others to make you happy. Your happiness is solely up to you. We all have the potential for great happiness because whatever our circumstances, the decision to be happy is still up to us. This was one of the most difficult aspects of life that I had to learn. I had never known true happiness growing up so it was difficult to accept the fact that my happiness was up to me. I had developed a critical judgmental spirit from living in a violent dysfunctional home. I had fun times running and playing with my brothers and sisters, but peace and happiness always eluded me. I could not control my childhood circumstances, but now I have a choice. I no longer look to others to find my happiness. It is up to me.

Martin Seligman describes in his book, *Authentic Happiness*, how he conducted a study with a group of nuns and their lifespan. Interestingly, the nuns who lived the longest were the happiest and held the most positive feelings and outlook on life. Unhappy people were more introspective and spent more time alone. Happy people have more close friends and are involved more with groups. Those who held positive optimistic feelings and engaged in humor tended to live a longer, more fulfilled life. Pessimists, on the other hand, were more apt to be jealous and paranoid and live shorter lives. Each seemed to view the world differently, but the real truth here is that happier people tend to live longer healthier lives. It is important to identify your strengths and not focus on your weakness.

Reliving and rehashing our unhappy experiences and how life is unfair is a sure way to remain miserable. We blame our job, spouse, kids, and extended family for injustices and causing our anger and distress. Did you ever consider that it might lie within you—perhaps you are fueling your own anger and nurturing your own problem? However, the question still remains, how can we fix it? How can we find happiness in a never-ending cycle of misery, why is this happening and will it ever end?

You must get outside yourself and observe, like you were doing a critique—only it is you who is being analyzed. Ask yourself why you are so angry? What triggers this underlying anger and resentment? Disappointments, pain and suffering is the way of human existence. Everyone has setbacks and disappointments; the difference is in how it is perceived and translated in the mind. Continually hanging on to past mistakes or injustices will keep you a prisoner of the past. Accepting change is the first step toward healing resentment. Change will affect everyone at different times in their lives— friendships and jobs change, locations change, our health or the health of loved ones can change; it is inevitable but it does not have to rule over your happiness.

I finally came to a point in my life where I realized that it was now time for me to take responsibility for my own life and happiness. I could not continue blaming my past for my lack of joy in the present. I began to understand that I was keeping the pain of my past alive by focusing on injustices I experienced as a child. It was only in letting go and taking my focus off my past that I was able to find peace and joy in the present.

Happiness comes from within us and trying to access it through our partner or spouse will never provide security and acceptance. It is not his job to make you happy and he should not be expected to change to please you. Nor should he be trying to change you in order to meet his needs. I am not saying that there might be areas you both could work on to create a stronger union between the two of you. Leave the poor guy alone and work on you! The more you attempt to force change in him, the wider the gulf between you will grow.

The following is a quote I recently read in an online article in *Fox News Magazine*. "Many women who are dating after a divorce (or any time) don't respect men. They don't value, like or appreciate men. You can tell by how they speak about men— both the new men they meet, and the ones from their past." There is no question that divorce, cheating, controlling and physically abusing women do happen, and being mistreated can cause many women to become cynical. However, continually bashing men will draw the same type of man you are complaining about. Maybe it is time to embrace a new entertainment by finding qualities in men that you are attracted to instead of the negative ones.

Reinforcing your partner and praising his qualities might inspire him to have a desire toward pleasing you. If you constantly criticize and point out his flaws, you will draw more conflict into your life. No one wants to be accused and attacked by the person who professes to love them. Sometimes conflict can simply be misunderstandings or unrealistic expectations. If you feel driven to constantly challenge your partner's motivation, you are setting the stage for more destructive behavior. The curtain will come down as he runs for cover. He will erect a wall of protection around himself and shut you out!

Women have shared with me over the years that finding the right man to love would make them happy. They are still searching for someone to find passion and excitement and live a life of bliss. However, unless the relationship is built on an inner exchange of likes and dislikes and a mutual respect for each other's values, there may be serious troubles ahead. Sooner or later, passion rides off into the sunset and with no sound foundation to hold the union together, divorce may soon be galloping right behind it.

Cleo's Story

For 30 years, I tolerated my husband's outbursts of anger. The slightest aggravation would trigger violent fits of screaming, yelling, cursing and threatening. I was finding it increasingly difficult to even speak to him or converse for any reason as I did not want to provoke his anger. Even though he had never physically hit me, I was always terrified of his uncontrolled verbal abuse.

After I retired and was around him more, his screaming escalated to every day and night at the slightest aggravation. One day, I just simply could not take it anymore. I found a furnished apartment and moved my things out of our home. He was shocked and pleaded with me to give him one more chance. I just walked out and shut the door.

I was away for several months when my mother died. We had been very close and she was my only family. I was devastated and grieved to the point of getting sick. My husband called frequently and suggested that I move back home where he could take care of me. When I refused, he began crying and pleaded with me to come home for just two weeks; I could return to my apartment any time I wanted. I agreed and must admit that I was never treated more respectfully in my entire life. I had always been accommodating in the past and thought that would create more love in him. Nothing I tried to do to appease him worked.

I did not fully trust this "changed man" image he attempted to portray. I was afraid it was a façade and eventually his old unhappy self would emerge. He really seemed changed and assured me that he had had a lot of time to reflect and grieve when I left him and was deeply sorry. He said he would spend the rest of his life making it up to me. I did not know what to say to him. I was so overcome by his remarks but the fear and apprehension still felt present.

After the two weeks went by, he once again begged me not to leave. He stated that he could not bear living life without me and he proposed a plan to take a trip together and start over. I reluctantly agreed to go but about half way through our trip, he began to revert back to his old ways. Since it was a motor trip, he was free to yell and scream at me in the car, out of the range of other's ears. I was devastated.

Once we returned home, he calmed down again and made his worn-out feeble apologies. I did not say anything and found it difficult to even crawl into bed with him. We were home for a short time and the screaming began. The first time I was shocked and silent, but the second time was more that I could take. I have no idea where the strength came from but I turned around, faced him head on, stuck my finger in his face and said, "Don't you ever raise your voice to me again!" He blinked a couple of times and backed up and mumbled, "I will never do it again." He has never raised his voice to me since. I had tried so hard to make him happy and all I accomplished was compromising myself and giving him all the power.

Why did I wait so long to confront him? I really don't know, but I think maybe down deep I thought I could make him happy and this would change his behavior. I am still with him and he acts like a deflated balloon. I believe his low self-esteem was bolstered by abusing and bullying me. No one ever saw him abusing me. He was so full of hatred and such a coward that he only did it behind closed doors. I finally understood that I am not responsible for his happiness, but I am responsible for mine, and his insufferable behavior will never again be tolerated! I just wish I would have stood up to him thirty years ago!

I was happy that Cleo was finally able to confront that destructive relationship, but I feel sad for her when I think of the wasted years spent with an unhappy angry man. Had Cleo challenged her husband's verbal abuse years ago, she may have had a more fulfilling life. Instead, for years, she silently tolerated his fits of rage before finally having the courage to confront him.

Cruel, harsh, and critical words will take their toll on any relationship. Creating an environment of verbal abuse not only affects our self-esteem but our physical health as well. If you are living a pattern of disrespect towards your spouse, children or extended family, you need to "quit" right now and stop this abuse. One day you may find yourself in a very lonely place as no one will want to be in your presence. There is nothing to gain by engaging in this inappropriate behavior. What if you were raised in a screaming battling household; get over it and stop the cycle now!

In Eckhart Tolle's book, *The Power of Now*, he brilliantly explains the 'Now' or as I like to call it, *living in the moment*. It is a heady read and I often found myself shaking my head saying, "What?" But as I began digesting the truth behind the Now, I slowly started to understand. It is okay to have memories of your past and reflect on those events, as long as you don't attempt to make the past your Now. It is gone and nothing you can say or do can ever bring it back.

Perhaps your past was traumatic like mine and you do not ever want to go there again. However, if you are letting your mind control your thoughts, it will continue to do what it has been programmed to do. Eckhart Tolle explains that our mind likes to keep control and run the show, but we have the right to take back our power. The only reality we have is this very moment, not yesterday or tomorrow, but Now! The same is true for our future. We can plan and promote and become anxious about anticipated results, but the future will eventually become this very moment, the Now. Imagine yourself with space moving out from you like our expanding universe. Allow each moment to fill that space.

Don't live your life with regrets for the *"road not taken."* There is no way you will ever know where you might have ended up had you taken the other road. You have to live with the road you did choose. Suffering a remorseful existence will never allow you to go back in time and take a journey down that other road. However, living your present life with regrets of the unknown will breed even greater disappointment. You now have new choices to make as to which road you will take—that old road is gone. With a constant stream of negative thoughts and emotions about your past, there is no room for peace and happiness in your life. We must learn to "Let It Be." Answers will come if we just *let it be.* Look at it, observe it and then leave it alone—give it no life.

I began researching the art of happiness and for all the information available today, I found very little help other than changing my attitude. How do we change our attitude when it is the only one we have ever known? There had to be more to this than attitude. I thought maybe it would help to just ignore negative feelings and not give them any life. Still, they lurked in the back of my mind, waiting to chant their inner voice.

In my search I came across a book, *The Art of Happiness, 10th Anniversary Edition, A Handbook for Living*, by His Holiness the Dalai Lama and Howard C. Cutler, M.D. Reading this book opened up an entirely new view and concept for true happiness. Here is the Dali Lama's formula for happiness in a few short words. *"If you want others to be happy, practice compassion; and if you want yourself to be happy, practice compassion."* Compassion? Really? Will practicing compassion actually make us happy? It seemed to me that if we went about feeling compassion for everyone we encountered, we might become depressed at our helplessness. This was a whole new concept for me and I determined the only way I could decide if it was true was to try it out for myself.

I was a dismal failure in practicing compassion. I really was not certain what to do. I decided I would just try to be more open and accepting of others by smiling more and making eye contact. I noticed in doing this that most people don't smile often; however, when I made it a habit of projecting warm feelings of gratitude from my heart, I finely began to understand the happiness and compassion relationship.

The Dalai Lama also stresses that along with compassion is the need for acceptance. I am not referring to just doing kind acts or offering consoling words, as you may come across as condescending. I decided to try his approach the next time I was with a group of friends. I followed the Dalai Lama's instruction to meditate and focus beforehand with a clear purpose, to be kind and caring and, above all, real. How do we begin practicing compassion? Try observing the person or persons you are with and ask yourself: *What do they need at this moment and what can I say or do that might be helpful?* Compassion is actually expressing kindness and acceptance.

You will be amazed at the sense of connection you will feel toward them. This approach lets down their barriers and allows you inside their inner sanctum. They may open just a tiny crack to peek out of but it is a start toward acceptance as they begin to feel safe and less vulnerable. Eckhart Tolle says: *"Compassion is the awareness of a deep bond between yourself and all creation."* Thinking thoughts of compassion is far different from feeling sorry for someone. People do not want your pity; they want your acceptance. This instills in others a sense of meaning and connection. Perhaps they feel validated in their soul for the first time in their life. Don't wait for others to reach out in compassion to you, practice reaching out first and then watch the magic begin! This is what His Holiness the Dali Lama says: *"If you maintain a feeling of compassion, loving kindness, then something automatically opens your inner door. Through that you can communicate much more easily with other people."* Compassion not only opens their inner door but it opens yours as well!

Will everyone respond to you? No, probably not. Their state of inner negativity and anger might be so ingrained that they feel safe with the familiar, closely held darkness. They do not yet have the capacity to allow even a tiny slit to expand their space or let their light shine out for all to see. As you continue to express more compassion in a genuine and loving way, they may begin to allow you into their inner sanctum. If nothing more, they will be drawn to your acceptance of them.

Our society is full of people just longing to fit in and be accepted. They feel alone and having someone connect with them in a meaningful engaging way can make so much difference in their world. Be careful that you do not close out potential friendships because you misinterpreted shyness for aloofness. Many have spent a good portion of their lives feeling rejected and are still protecting themselves from past pain by keeping their inner door tightly locked.

My husband and I were having dinner with a male friend who was dating again after a year of being single. We enquired how this new scene was working for him. His reply was surprising. He said, "As soon as I ask a woman out and we have an enjoyable dinner together, she tries to latch on and begins calling me almost daily." He said at first it was rather flattering and then it became downright annoying. "When I try to break it off, they insist I tell them what they did wrong. It is very embarrassing as I don't want to hurt anyone."

Now this is the shocking truth of our evening out with our single friend. At ten o'clock, as we were paying our dinner checks, his cell phone rang and, without having to ask any questions, it was totally clear as to the nature of the call. He said, "Oh well, no, if you want to see me, you should come to my place because I have to feed and walk my dog, and then I would have to drive out of my way to get to your house and it would be too late." All the while, he was rolling his eyes at us to express his boredom and indifference to the invitation. I began to tease him and commented that when a man calls a woman late at night, it is known as a *booty call*. He laughed and said, "That is what guys call it too. You know perfectly well, Barbara, when a woman calls a man at ten o'clock on a Friday night to come over to her house, she has expectations."

I asked him why he had not invited her to dinner with us and he said, "I didn't feel like it and we are not in an exclusive relationship. I don't really feel like having her come over either as I already know she won't leave and will stay the night." Wow! How embarrassing! If you are a woman reading this and you are doing anything close to what I have just described, you need to stop. Also, be assured that he will not respect you and will eventually tire of you and your neediness and you will go to the curb. Do you really want to be somebody's joke over dinner, or do you want to find a man who will treat you with dignity and honor? You must start by first treating yourself with dignity and honor, as a princess would. Don't think for a minute that I believe it is okay for a man to accept the late-night call and not a woman, because I don't support that at all.

I told him exactly how I felt and how unfair it is to lead her on or encourage her to remain in a relationship that is purely one sided. A princess deserves a much better deal than this.

Don't chase down a man no matter how much you want to talk to him, see him, hang out or go out with him. This is like begging for love and affection. If he senses your neediness and desperation, he will run; he will say, "Let me out of here!" Men are biologically designed to be warriors, hunter gatherers, and conquerors. When you assume their role—you lose! You may succeed in catching him, but you still lose the game, because he will not give you the love and attention you crave. You made it way too easy for him.

In order to develop a happy attitude, it is important to align your self-image with the power of positive thinking. The two must be going down the same path in order to create change. This is determined only by you and the goals you have set for yourself. You can intellectually tell yourself that you are going to change but in order to align with your intellect; you must willfully decide and practice change.

We have learned from experiments with basketball players that focusing intently and imagining shooting baskets over and over again brought the same results as the players who were physically on the court playing the game. However, in order for the player imagining shooting baskets to get the best results, she had to totally and completely see the ball going through the hoop. It was important to feel it as she shot the ball and see it as it entered the hoop. Then the mental player had to feel the sense of satisfaction and excitement, knowing she had shot a basket.

The same process is true for us in order to create change in our own lives. First, we imagine it then we shoot for it and feel the satisfaction as we reach our goals! We all have an image of ourselves. The image began in childhood, based on our experiences. We have created our own belief system whether we are aware of it or not and we lead our lives according to our beliefs. When I was in counseling with Hugh, one of the most valuable truths he taught me was when he said, "The truest thing about you, Barbara, is not what you were taught to believe as a child, but what God says about you. The King of the universe says you are his child and that makes you a princess!" The way we act, feel and behave becomes consistent with our self-image. You will act and behave on the self-image you have been programmed to believe from youth until you decide to change it.

How can we implement change and break this destructive cycle? Wishing for a change or even knowing you should change does not bring it about until your self-conception changes. Deciding that your life will never change because you have tried to instigate change many times before is simply nodding approval and giving recognition to failure and power to your past. Expand your comfort zone. Each time you allow space to expand outward away from you—you grow and your power increases. Your protective cellophane wrap will be powerless to hold you in. It is time to bust loose and dare to take action. The push through power lies within you; it is just waiting for you to release it.

There are good reasons to be happy. A Mayo Clinic study done on 2282 participants over 65 years of age and living in the southwestern United States showed that the happiest individuals were less likely to die early or become age-disabled.

Positive emotions played a major role in who lived the longest and were the happier people. The study also revealed that the immune systems of happy people were more resistant to illness, weight gain and high blood pressure. This was not good news for the pessimistic group of individuals. It is wise to recognize if you have this attitude and seek out ways to be happy.

Everyone's act of kindness is different. Some might express compassion by visiting nursing homes, volunteering in a soup kitchen, driving a friend to chemo treatments, taking a meal to shut-ins, or donating money to a cause. Engaging in compassion and acts of kindness and expecting nothing in return is the true meaning of happiness.

Researchers tell us that happy people set higher goals and even have a better performance level. The more focused on positive emotions we become, the less room we allow for negative emotions. The optimist even attracted more positive friends and seemed to focus more and have more compassion in sharing and helping others. The unhappy or pessimistic people appeared to spend more time alone and have less interaction with others. Which would you prefer: happiness, good health, creativity and longevity, or pessimism, loneliness, ill health and irritability?

Along with compassion, we must learn to live in a state of gratitude. A spirit of gratitude can change our need to compare ourselves to others. What are you grateful for? Perhaps you are living in a difficult situation and being grateful is the farthest thought from your mind. Our current economy has many living in a state of numbness and depression. Watching the news is enough to send us back to bed to wait for better times.

I was returning home from one of my walks to the beach and decided to take the tram part way back. Our tram drivers are mostly older retired men. When I jumped off the tram, I said, "Thanks Joe, and have a great day!" He quickly replied, "I already have had a great day, I woke up!" I smiled the rest of the way home because I had just received a great dose of *gratitude*. When I think of these men, many of whom are retired professionals, out there in the Florida heat for hours each day, it makes me grateful and filled with compassion.

Barbara Miller

Negative States of Mind

There is an inner sanctum within each of us that holds our deepest desire and intention. Only we can unlock and open the door to illuminate the darkness and let our light shine out into the universe. Create space by opening up and expanding your compassion and allow your positive energy to flow outward to embrace others. The decision to ignore your negative attitude will only reinforce your unhappiness. You might be ignoring it by turning a blind eye at who you are hurting and how that impacts others. Choosing to remain in a dark place will only breed more of the same.

The more focus we give our problems, the more power they hold over us. Finding a way to take the attention away from our problems takes them out of the limelight. Focusing on the needs of another and what challenges they may be experiencing can shift our thoughts away from ourselves. There are myriad numbers of individuals who have many more challenges, problems, and obstacles to overcome than you might have. Feeling compassion for the suffering of others is what the Dali Lama teaches is the way to happiness.

There are numerous examples in the Bible of Jesus having compassion on the crowds who thronged to him for healing. Could he have healed them without compassion or was it a deep desire to see them whole both physically and spiritually that gave energy to the healing? I believe it was both.

Don't make your happiness dependent on outside conditions and circumstances. You will create a cycle of anticipation followed by disappointment. You must cultivate your state of happiness from within and break the cycle of frustration and anxiety. Your own personal happiness must never depend on another person. What they say or do should never be the criteria for your happiness. Is it any wonder we are all burned out, stressed out, and exhausted? We have been taught to lead a phony life of *fitting in*.

What would happen if you stepped out of line took a break and walked out into the bright light of day and decided from that point on to live your life from the inside out instead of from the outside in? Host your own celebration as to who you truly are— a shining light of the Universe—a fearless Warrior Princess!

Here are a few guidelines that I discovered in my research. Try writing down each day for 10 days at least three specific things you are thankful for. This will be a great opportunity to really reflect on what you have such as friendships, a loving spouse, amazing kids, a warm home, or cool for that matter, a car—think of all the people in the world who walk everywhere. How about books, the internet and all the resources we have available to gain knowledge, and freedom of religion. I am certain you will have a different list than mine for all the wonderful things in your life you have to be thankful for.

- Live in the moment.
- Resist competing by attempting to keep with others. Compete only with yourself.
- Develop caring relationships.

- Share what you have with others; time, talent and treasure.
- Open up your heart to receive love.
- Resist the urge to always have the last word; quiet down and listen.
- Laugh and make optimism a daily habit. Move it and do it regularly and preferably with someone.

Research has shown that exercise can beat the blues and be as effective for treating depression as prescription drugs. The feel-good endorphins provide a healthy dose of contentment and even give your self-esteem a boost. When you are happy, you send out positive vibrations into the Universe. Own your happiness and recognize where it resides—inside of you!

> *"The real purpose of life is just to be happy—to enjoy life. To get to a place where you are not always trying to get some-place else. So many people spend their lives striving, trying to be someplace that they're not, they never get to arrive."* Dr. Wayne Dyer

Chapter 7
DANCE OF HEALTH

"In order to live more fully, to meet the stressors and challenges of life (including fear, panic, and anxiety) more effectively, and to embrace the wonder and awe of life more completely, it is fundamental that each of us learns to connect with and dwell in the present moment." Jeffery Brantley, MD, *Calming Your Anxious Mind.*

Tickled Pink

Laughter is one of life's most profound health benefits. Laughter is a great release from stress and anxiety, which strengthens your immune system. According to Dr. Rashid A. Buttar, author of *The 9 Steps to Keep the Doctor Away: Simple Actions to Shift Your Body and Mind to Optimum Health for Greater Longevity*: *"Laughter stimulates the lymphatic system, increases lung capacity and dilates blood vessels, allowing you to feed and regenerate your cells and efficiently eliminate waste and toxins from your body."* Wow, all the more reason to laugh loud and often. Besides, laughter is contagious so you can help transfer laughter's entire multitude of benefits to others just by engaging them in infectious laughter! Laughter triggers the release of endorphins which helps make you feel good, soothes pain and helps protect your heart.

Practice laughing out loud at least six times a day. David began to think I was losing my mind when he kept hearing me laughing while sitting at my computer. I decided to practice laughing so I had to find something to laugh about. I found jokes or funny stories on the internet. Some of those annoying mass emails friends send can actually be quite funny. Whenever you are tempted to be critical, find something to praise or laugh about. My grandfather used to tease my grandmother by tickling her and tweaking her cheeks. She would scold and order him to stop and he would grin and say, "No, I won't quit." Finally, she would succumb to his unrelenting tickling, knowing that the only way to get him to stop was to lighten up and laugh.

Laughter truly is the best tonic for our soul. Getting together with fun, happy people is as invigorating as a two-mile walk. Nothing makes me feel better than deep, from-the-gut laughter! Laughter suppresses the stress hormone levels of epinephrine and cortisol, while at the same time boosting the body's natural levels of endorphins. Step out of your comfort zone and take some risk. Act silly—it's okay to laugh at yourself.

One of the happiest people I know is my Aunt Janette. She is my father's youngest sister and only one year older than me and one year younger than my sister Carol. The three of us grew up together laughing. One of the most fun things about visiting Aunt Janette was that she had a horse. We had a way of coaxing him over to the fence by giving him an apple. We were perched and already standing on the fence ready to jump on and go for a ride. I was the smallest and was happy to be in the middle. When our ride tired of us, he simply lowered his head and leaned forward until we slid down his neck to the ground. We would giggle and laugh and run off to find some other entertainment. That happy memory is locked in my heart forever.

One of the things I miss most in living apart from my family is spending time together just laughing. I especially loved Thanksgiving with my siblings at my sister Carol's house. Oh, how we did laugh! It was just a continuous roar of laughter. After lunch, the women did the dishes and cleaned up while the men disappeared as fast as they could to watch the football games. The minute we finished in the kitchen, we headed straight back to the dining room table to tell tales and laugh ourselves silly. I believe our gift of laughter was a healing catalyst that helped us through some trying times. We were still sitting at the table when it was time to eat again. Laughter even boosts your immune system. Another benefit to laughter is that men are attracted to happy women. If you want to feel better about your life and improve your health, laugh and laugh often.

Every time I remember an event that took place many years ago, I still laugh. We were visiting Disney World in Orlando, Florida, and two boys discovered that when one held their finger over the water spout on the drinking fountain, the water would come out of another fountain much higher. Well, you can imagine the scenario as the boys figured out that this was a great prank to play on unsuspecting thirsty visitors. We watched for several minutes as one after another got a face full of water and those who spotted the tricksters in action burst into spontaneous laughter. Before long, a crowd had gathered and everyone exchanged rounds of laughter at the spectacle. I am certain that all of those who shared in the laughter had even more fun that day at Disney World. I know we sure did. The feel-good endorphins were having their own great party!

A few years ago, my sister Deb and I travelled to Miami, Florida, to attend a spa and skin care show. I still had my spa in Michigan and loved to attend the Miami show for information on new trends and products for my clients. After hours and hours of walking from booth to booth, we decided to purchase a facial mask product that when applied, it appeared as if you had had a face lift. We were excited as we headed back to the hotel to test out our new product. Deb carefully read the directions as she was going to apply the product on my face. Start with a clean dry face, then briefly soak the individual mask pieces in warm water, then apply them to the face. You started with the forehead, then under the eyes, separate pieces for cheeks, above and below lips. Next, a large piece was applied to my neck. The instructions said to leave the mask on for 30 minutes and do not talk as this would cause the strips to lift.

It was a perfect time for a nap. Deb was going to read so she could wake me up to take of my mask. About two hours later, I woke up with a shock as I did not know where I was and I could not move my mouth. I tried to scream but if you ever saw the Wizard of Oz where the Tin Man's mouth was rusted shut and he is trying to tell Dorothy he needed his oil can, my sound was similar. My sister had fallen asleep and when she heard my muffled sound, she flew to my side screaming "No, oh no!" She could not peel the mask off because it had dried like cement. The only alternative was a very wet, warm towel to soak the pieces off. I just lay there, wondering if my face had disappeared. By now, Deb was laughing hysterically and I felt like if I laughed, my face would crack. Finally, the pieces were all off and I could dare to look in the mirror. We laughed until it hurt and my face, although very pink, looked amazing!

Barbara Miller

Massage Benefits

Massage is a language unto its own. We as humans have been nurtured by touch from birth. History has revealed that babies who were not touched or nurtured by human contact did not thrive and many did not live long. The healing touch of massage is thousands of years old and in many parts of Europe, massage is prescribed by doctors to treat an ailing patient. For several years, massage seemed a lost art, only available in seedy massage parlors with questionable masseurs or masseuses. Massage therapy has evolved once again and is now widely accepted as a respectable profession in spite of the recent bad press involving the rich and famous.

There are numerous types of massage: Swedish, Shiatsu, Sport Massage, Reflexology and Mindfulness massage such as Reiki. In Mindfulness massage, the therapist works closely with the energy field surrounding both the client and the therapist. Some are uncomfortable with this type of connection and prefer a more traditional massage. Whichever style is right for you, massage has many benefits. It helps control blood pressure, ease arthritis pain and soothe muscle pain from fibromyalgia, not to mention that it feels heavenly and at times puts me to sleep.

Whether your massage of choice works mainly with the muscles or is concentrated on the pressure points of the body, there are health benefits as each type of massage promotes the body's own self-healing ability. Touch is developed at birth and is vital to a sense of well-being, nurture, and acceptance. Even as adults, there is a need to connect and hug and feel human touch. The degree of touching throughout our developing years plays a major role in our self-esteem.

Massage has been in practice for thousands of years and is even visible in paintings in Egyptian tombs. The Romans and Greeks used massage as a means to heal the sick. The father of medicine, Hippocrates, wrote, *"The Physician must be experienced in many things, but assuredly in rubbing. For rubbing can bind a joint that is too loose, and loosen a joint that is too rigid."* Unfortunately, our "don't touch me" American culture rejected this ancient healing technique called *massage* until recent years. Treat yourself and your wellbeing to a therapeutic massage and reap its many benefits.

Get Brainy

Your body is not the only thing that needs exercise to stay fit. Your brain also needs a healthy workout. Those who have careers and daily work challenges show less mental decline than those who sit home in front of the television most of the day and night. Staying mentally engaged plays a major role in warding off dementia. No, watching television is not active stimulation; it is passive and does nothing to preserve cognitive function. Have a group of friends over and play bridge. This way you not only challenge your brain but you get the healthy benefits of laughter and interaction. Studies confirm that having a social network of friendships plays a major role in overall mental function. Close friendships can even affect our immune system and reduce illness such as the common cold and help reduce blood pressure.

I have personally had a lifelong love affair with learning new things. I am currently studying health and wellness through an online college. This is a great way to wake up your brain and pull your thinking cap out of mothballs. Learning any type of new information will help prevent cognitive decline. The old *use it or lose it* still applies and your brain loves to be stimulated. Your brain will actually shrink if you do not use it. Our bodies change as we age and so does the brain. The cerebral cortex, the brain's outer layer, grows thinner over time. Since this is the area where we process information and what decisions to make, we need to protect our brain. Well, the good news is that studies have shown that those who meditate have a thicker cerebral cortex. Think of how you get bored just sitting around doing nothing; well, so does your brain get bored. Hopefully, you are not keeping your brain in a "yawn state."

A study by researchers at Rush University Medical Center in Chicago, Illinois, showed that you can counteract the effects of Alzheimer's disease by having goals and purpose. Having meaning and interest in your life can reduce cognitive decline by up to 30 per cent. Even if you already have early signs of Alzheimer's disease, having a positive attitude and living a purposeful life promotes cognitive health.

I have also been studying social media and how to use it to promote my book. There are so many new and exciting social media sites online that I have to limit just how many I want to spend time learning and visiting. There is absolutely no reason to sit around bored with your brain in neutral. Take a computer class or buy an iPhone and actually learn how to use it. You can even learn how to play numerous games on the internet. The brain loves anything new that challenges it to think. Consider it like calisthenics to strengthen and give your brain a workout.

Butt Out

Quit smoking; it's a no-brainer. It is not just your business if you smoke; it is the business of everyone you come in contact with. The impact your habit has on your children could influence them to mimic you and start smoking. Smoking deeply affects your lungs and heart. My father smoked three packs of Camels a day and died at 49 years of age from an aortic aneurism. The first question the doctor asked was if he smoked. Smoking narrows the blood vessels and compromises blood flow throughout the body. This puts tremendous strain on your heart and can lead to a stroke. Smoking can even cause bladder cancer many years after you have quit as well as being a risk factor for periodontal disease.

Your second-hand smoke can harm everyone around you; not to mention if you become ill. My mother's sister, my Aunt Lillian who used to send me the beautiful play clothes when I was a child, died of lung cancer. Aunt Lillian was beautiful but her deadly habit of two or three packs of cigarettes per day cost her dearly. She was very independent, never had children, and saw no reason to quit smoking because it was her business and she enjoyed it. Well, guess what; it was no longer "her business" when she became too sick to take of herself and my mother and family had to take turns caring for her. Do yourself a favor and quit before it is too late to undo the damage.

Barbara Miller

Get Some Zzz's

Sleep deprivation is a growing concern in our modern world. There are so many distractions that keep us pumped up and hyped up that it seems nearly impossible to calm down and just plain relax. Our homes are like an arcade—with flashing computers, televisions, cells phones, digital clocks, and sounding beepers on our washers and dryers! Help me, please! It is no wonder our circadian rhythms are all messed up. The body doesn't know if it is morning, noon or night; whether to wind down or get primed for a busy day.

I have struggled with insomnia for the last ten years and I truly sympathize with those of you who can't seem to get enough sleep. I have started practicing Mindfulness meditation and it has made a tremendous difference in my ability to go to sleep and stay asleep. I was only averaging four hours of sleep per night. I could not seem to stop my thoughts enough to relax and fall asleep and so spent the majority of my days exhausted and foggy. It was like I was running on half empty and in slow motion. Those of you who suffer insomnia are familiar with this feeling. I finally allowed my doctor to prescribe a mild sedative because I knew I could not go on indefinitely without adequate sleep. However, I discovered that I had traded one problem for another because even though I was sleeping, I felt drugged and sluggish the next day.

I began researching meditation online and learned about the Silva Method which teaches that you must learn to take control of your thoughts instead of allowing your thoughts to control you. The Silva Method was designed by Jose Silva and is a self-help program intended to promote a sense of wellbeing through relaxation and visualization. The Silva Method uses guided imagery and focused awareness to help zero in and gain clarity on your goals. I have noticed a definite sense of calmness. I no longer take the prescribed sedative and I feel a stronger sense of well-being. I am sleeping longer and better and feel more rested; however, if you are on a prescribed medication, please consult with your doctor before deciding to stop taking it. There are various types of meditation and you may want to do your own research to find one that works for you.

I just finished reading *Calming Your Anxious Mind, How Mindfulness and Compassion Can Free You from Anxiety, Fear and Panic*, by Jeffery Brantley, MD. Being mindful is simply being present in the moment. Doctor Brantley explains how to make the present moment your reality; not your past, not your future—but your awareness of NOW. Mindfulness meditation is like being a silent observer watching your thoughts, but not being your thoughts. If you really want to learn about the various meditations and which might work for you, I highly recommend Dr. Brantley's book, *Calming Your Anxious Mind.*

Dial down the temperature in your bedroom to no higher than 75 degrees Fahrenheit. According to the National Sleep Foundation, having a routine sleep schedule provides better sleep. I absolutely cannot get to sleep without socks. Studies have shown that if your head or your feet are too cold, it might impair your ability to relax and thus miss quality sleep. Toss the television out of the bedroom. Consider it an interloper to your intimate space. If your partner wants to watch a late-night program and you really need sleep, this will only lead to dissention and the bedroom is the last place you need conflict. Noise pollution is a big issue these days with televisions, computers, phones, and alarms. We all need to turn off, dial down, and get some rest. I am hard line about no television, computer, or phone in the bedroom and my husband has never objected. With countless intrusions clamoring for our attention, our bedroom needs to be our haven.

We should also take some tips from other countries throughout the world that still close up shop for *siesta time.* I used to think it was a strange custom and in certain countries like Spain, you might as well take a little nap yourself because the shops are all closed early afternoon for *siesta time.*

Now that I understand the positive impact this has on overall health, I think it is a custom we should adopt. I visit the country of Panama frequently and my dentist in Panama actually closes his office for two hours at lunch time and goes home, gets his pajamas on and crawls into bed for his nap. I love it!

Tapping

No, I am not referring to tap dancing. Meridian Tapping is similar to acupuncture without the needles. Dr. George Goodheart, Dr. John Diamond and Dr. Roger Callahan were all instrumental in developing tapping techniques. Dr. Goodheart discovered that he could get the same results by tapping on acupuncture points. Patients' overall well-being was enhanced by this practice. Tapping was considered a complicated technique until a student of Dr. Callahan, Gary Craig, developed

EFT or Emotional Freedom Technique. EFT has since become the leading tapping technique.

EFT is actually ancient, but has evolved to modern forms. It is similar to acupuncture but without the use of needles. Tapping on what are known as energy meridians helps to release trapped emotional problems. There is a sequence to tapping on acupressure points of the body. Tapping is used in conjunction with positive affirmations to unblock past trauma, addiction, and pain, thus opening up pathways that allow electromagnetic energy to flow freely through the body and restore balance. You can read more about EFT on Nick Ortner's website at: www.thetappingsolution.com.

Tai Chi

Tai Chi is a slow deliberate physical exercise practiced by the Chinese for at least 2500 years. My girlfriend Patti and I visited Hong Kong together in 1990. Hong Kong is much like New York City with its high rises, millions of people, and not a lot of open space. Our hotel was in an older area with apartments and small shops. On our first morning in Hong Kong, Patti woke me up excitedly. "Barbara, get up and come to the window, there are hundreds of people everywhere doing some sort of slow dance." I flew to the window and witnessed this amazing phenomenon for the first time. They were practicing Tai Chi, from the very old to the very young, on every square foot of space.

Tai Chi is a slow, graceful, meditative exercise that promotes strength and inner peace. Even though Tai Chi draws on internal energy, it is a martial art and uses the body's energy much like meridian tapping. This exercise and meditative discipline bring the body into balance and allows its energy to flow freely. Tai Chi should be done in a graceful seamless flow. Many health clubs now offer Tai Chi.

Research has shown that practicing Tai Chi for eight weeks improves balance and flexibility, thus reducing fear of falling. It strengthens both mind and body as it takes focus and concentration to learn and practice the movements. This appears to reduce stress in the body and relieve arthritis pain. You do not need a lot of space to practice Tai Chi as I witnessed on my trip to Hong Kong. Hundreds of people were on hillsides, in parks and even in the markets, all practicing Tai Chi. The internet abounds with instructions and information on this wonderful Chinese practice. It is a great way to lower blood pressure, strengthen your body and increase a sense of wellbeing.

Yoga

Yoga originated in India and in Sanskrit it is considered a physical, mental and spiritual discipline. Sanskrit Yoga means union of body, mind, and spirit. Yoga is similar to Tai Chi as both develop strength and flexibility. There are many types of yoga classes offered and you may want to visit a few studios to find a suitable style. If you have never tried yoga before, I suggest starting in a beginner's class with a knowledgeable instructor. I started a class that was promoted as intermediate and I was way out of my league, not to mention that I could barely move the next day. I need to work up to twisting into a pretzel and doing the splits! Oh my! I was the one as a child who was so skinny and gangly, I could never even turn a cartwheel, let alone do a backbend!

I recently learned that my local WMCA offered yoga and Pilates combined and they call it YoPli. I joined the class and absolutely love it, and the results have been amazing. I feel so energized when I leave class, I can accomplish so much more, and the real bonus is it seems to lessen aches and pains. Plus, I have met some amazing people!

I have been happy to learn about mindfulness and therapeutic Viniyoga. Duke University along with Aetna Insurance have conducted a study comparing therapeutic yoga with mindfulness meditation and had amazing results in regards to sleep and relaxation. For people who wanted natural ways to treat their insomnia, this was an answer and there were no side effects. Well, actually there were side effects but only good ones like quality sleep, lower blood pressure, less stress, and reduce pain. Search out a qualified Mindfulness-Based Stress Reduction (MBSR) instructor offering classes in your area and learn to relax and get some sleep.

Shall We Dance

A great way to give yourself a cardiac workout and flood your body with amazing feel-good hormones is to dance! No one has to teach a child how to dance; they just instinctively know how to move to the music. My husband David and I had great fun watching our grandson Jacob dancing to music when he was barely old enough to stand up. He crawled over to one of our speakers, pulled himself up, kept his hands on the speaker and began to shake his little diaper bottom to the beat.

Dancing gives the entire body a healthy workout, from the lungs to the limbs. I have always loved to dance and when my sister Carol and I came home from church one day and announced that our pastor told us we were not allowed to dance; yes, this is the same pastor who was later kicked out of the church for having an affair, my parents said, "No way! We have always danced and you kids are going to dance as well." We were so happy because we loved to watch American Bandstand and it seemed so unfair that we could no longer enjoy dancing. My father said we wore out the living room carpeting from rock-n-roll! We loved telling our friends that our parents made us dance. Guess whose house all the neighbor kids came to?

If you love dance and don't have a dance partner, you may want to check out Zumba. This great Columbian exercise is a combination of dance and aerobics. Zumba, pronounced zoomba, was created by Alberto "Beto" Perez, a celebrity fitness trainer. Beto had forgotten his aerobic CD for his class one day and had a CD of Columbian music he decided to use and voila! Zumba was born!

According to Wikipedia, over 12 million people take Zumba classes weekly, and I am one of them! That makes for a lot of happy hormones surging through millions of bodies every day! Zumba has many levels and because it is low impact, it appeals to all ages. Zumba is amazing for burning calories, about 1000 calories per hour! It is a great way to tone your body as well as rev up your metabolism. Rigorous dancing like Zumba stimulates the brain to create new cells and also strengthens your heart! I just joined a Zumba class at our local YMCA. Shake it up, baby!

It is not unusual to walk into a Zumba class and see your mother or grandmother doing their *"happy dance."* Zumba means move fast and have fun to of course, upbeat Latin music! If you are bored with treadmills and optical machines, make Zumba your own *"happy dance."* Some instructors mix it up a bit and combine resistance training. It is a great way to tone up the entire body as well as get the blood pumping! Inactivity is literally a killer. Slow down fat gain by keeping your body active. Zumba is amazing for trimming belly fat, so find a Zumba class near you and shake your booty—belly!

Healthy Resistance

I cannot begin to stress the value and long-term benefits of resistance training—specifically free weights. The benefits go far beyond the obvious—which is a toned and well-defined body. Weight lifting affects your entire body. If you depend on dieting alone and neglect weight bearing exercise, you will lose fat and valuable muscle. You will still have the same body, just smaller and weaker. This makes you far more likely to regain the weight and puts you on a path of yo-yo dieting.

Recently I went through a period of six weeks where I was unable to lift weights due to having had surgery. Shortly after

Barbara Miller

this time, my husband and I decided to take a trip on our boat. I had always been able to pull myself up onto the deck, but much to my surprise, I slid back down to the dock and had to try again. This took far more effort than it ever had before and I did not like the diminished way it made me feel. I became acutely aware of the muscle strength I had lost and I have to admit I was shocked. It was time to pick up the weights and get moving. Decline in muscle strength is one of the leading causes of falls as we age. Without muscle strength, our balance can also be affected, making it more difficult to recover after a fall.

I have exercised my entire life and lifted weights at least three times a week, and if I could actually lose strength in my arms that quickly, I cringe to think of the majority of women who do *nothing* to keep their body toned. The risk of falls and injuries are far greater to those who do not exercise. It is not just a toned body we are talking about here but quality of life, now and in the future. One in three people over age 65 will fall and for some who suffer broken bones, such as a hip fracture, may never walk again. Think about what that means for your future. I don't know about you but that gives me pause for concern. If you are not already doing routine walking, the time is now to get started and on alternate days, pick up those weights!

If you want to transform your body, resistance training along with aerobic exercise is the only way to keep your body strong and fit. I was hurrying through Sam's Club one day and stopped abruptly to help an older woman struggling to lift a 30-pound bag of dog food into her cart. I quickly reached down, grabbed the bag and placed it in her cart. "Wow," she exclaimed, how did you do that? You are much smaller than me." I said, "I can do that because I lift weights and you should too." She mumbled the usual excuses as I walked away to finish my own mission. Muscle strength is crucial to maintaining independence and 30 pounds is just not all that heavy, she should have been able to lift the bag of dog food herself. You simply cannot risk losing muscle tone as you age and there may not always be someone else to come to your rescue. Your quality of life will suffer.

There are so many benefits to lifting weights and maintaining a strong body. Think about what it means for your future. Your overall wellbeing is enhanced by weight lifting. Walking around with a hunched back or severely rounded shoulders from a deteriorating spine is a sure way to end up in a wheelchair. Weight lifting or resistance training is more critical than aerobic exercise. Weight lifting targets specific areas and helps to keep muscles toned and strong and enhances bone strength. Your bones desperately need strong muscles to support them. The strength of your frame is in the muscle! If you want to prevent falling, you must keep your legs strong through exercising your muscles.

The beauty of strength training is that you only have to do it three times a week for at least 20 minutes to 30 minutes and the tradeoff is strong, well-defined muscles! Find a trainer or knowledgeable friend to help you get started or even an online video can be your guide. You might want to check out the exercises with instructions on my website at: www.barbaraandcompany.com. They are simple weight lifting exercises and a great place to start if you have never lifted weights before. On alternate days, take time for a 30-minute power walk and walk fast enough to get your heart rate up so

Barbara Miller

you feel winded. Don't accept the old "it is in my genes" theory as to why you are gaining weight, and stop using it as an excuse. Of course, always check with your doctor before starting an exercise program.

I have a friend with an identical twin sister and I was shocked to meet the sister who was visiting from out of state. She was actually obese while her sister was a normal weight. My friend had shared with me how worried she was about her sister and was determined to keep her own weight in check. Both parents are obese and with serious health problems. She wanted to change their family belief system that excused their ill health as inevitable and blamed it on the genes.

Sally's Story

I came from a happy family and was blessed to have an identical twin sister. My parents were both obese and we were all fairly large boned, so it seemed normal to expect to look like everybody else. However, even at a young age, I knew I did not want to look like my mother. I loved her dearly and she was a wonderful mom and loved to bake and cook. When I became a teenager and really took notice of the copious amounts of food she consumed, I determined that I would pay more attention to what I put in my mouth. On the other hand, my sister Kelly followed mom's guide and began to put on weight.

I finished high school and went on to university, struggling to keep my weight stable. Some of my dorm friends used to get up early and when I asked what they were doing going out in the dark, they told me they were a running group. They invited me to join them and that began the odyssey of finally learning how to take charge of my body. I also learned from my new comrades how to eat properly to fuel my body and how to choose healthy snacks to keep in my dorm room instead of a bag of chips. Each time I saw my family after that first semester, they looked at me like I was a complete stranger. My sister was already tipping the scales at 200 pounds and began to distance herself from me whenever I came home. She dropped out of college and continued to live at home. I attempted to talk to her about what had happened to me at school but she just shrugged and went on eating.

I determined at that point that I could not control what decisions Kelly made for her life, but I definitely could control the decisions I made. During my senior year, I met a fabulous man and we have been happily married for 20 years. I have continued my running ever since my dorm friends invited me into their group and some of us still keep in touch. My sister also married and is still obese, along with her husband and two children. I wish I could do or say something to make her realize how she is compromising her life and the lives of those she loves, but she still turns a deaf ear. Our parents are both diabetics and my mother is now in a wheelchair. I refuse to let the genes excuse control my body and I am so grateful that a few dorm friends gave me the encouragement I needed to take charge of my life.

Bye Bye Belly

You owe it to yourself to know your waist-to-hip ratio. Fat around the middle, or what is known as an apple shape, is a sure invitation to heart disease. The problem with this type of fat is that it doesn't just sit there. It is active and secretes inflammatory compounds and toxins. This fat can actually choke out your other organs and lead to fatty liver disease. A Duke University study found that aerobic exercise done four times per week for 30 minutes reduced belly fat. However, the aerobic exercise had to be intense like jogging, power walking, biking, dancing or using a rowing machine. To check your waist to hip ratio; while standing, measure your waist and then measure your hips. Then divide your waist measurement by your hip measurement. It should not be over 0.8 for women or 0.9 for men.

If you live in an area where extreme weather may prevent outdoor walking or running, go to your local mall. There are plenty of mall walkers and I have seen them chatting and laughing while doing their mall laps. It is great exercise and it is good for the soul as well. Researchers at the University of Pittsburgh did a study on walkers and discovered that moderate exercise improves spatial memory. Older adults who walked three times a week for at least 40 minutes showed an increase in the size of the hippocampus. The sedentary adults showed shrinkage. Wow! Lace up those sneakers!

Go Mediterranean

Choosing to eat Mediterranean style is simply eating a colorful diet consisting of plant foods, fruit, nuts, fish, meat and healthy fats such as olive oil. There are myriad choices of fruits and vegetables depending on the area you live in to create your own Mediterranean-lifestyle eating. The key is to seek out whole fresh foods and avoid processed foods as much as possible. Condiments like salad dressings, ketchup and marinades are often loaded with salt and sugar. Generally, when producers have cut out the fat, it is replaced with sugar. Make your largest portion fruits and vegetables and add a small serving of fish or meat. Small portions mean an amount no bigger than a deck of cards. For variety, choose Greek style yogurt, cheese, eggs, olives, wine, and dark chocolate. Avoid deep frying and instead grill, broil, sauté or bake your food.

Try to buy fruits and vegetables that are in season for optimal freshness, and whenever possible, buy organic to avoid pesticides. Buying from local organic farmers is a great way to obtain the freshest and healthiest foods. Kids love to drive out in the country to pick apples, cherries, peaches, strawberries, and whatever else is in season. I used to take my daughter Alison with me to visit neighboring farms and purchase fruit and vegetables. It is such a fond memory for her that she now takes my two grandsons Jacob and Austin with her so they can build their own fond memories.

Keep eating out to a minimum, but it does not have to be your enemy. Make salad and vegetables the biggest part of your meal—not the bread and meat. Our American diets are an embarrassment and when I witness the copious amounts of food people consume in one meal, I am shocked! Everyone should be required to watch the movie about what is actually in the meat at McDonald's and just the fact that Chicken McNuggets are not even chicken is disgusting. This is a steady diet for thousands of children and adults who have no idea what they are eating.

Barbara Miller

I believe children need to be taught nutrition in school. If they are not learning good nutrition at home, chances are they will never learn it at all. American kids are now facing obesity at very young ages and it will compromise their lives and future. Many already suffer from diabetes and high cholesterol. Their high-fat diets full of snacks have literally no nutrition and put them at risk for heart disease. Obesity is now off the charts in America. This is a travesty! Most families eat while watching television and many never sit down together to share the day and enjoy each other. This creates mindless eating and may cause you to eat more than you need because you are distracted and focused on television and not your food.

Eat your breakfast! There have been enough studies done to make everyone aware that breakfast is the most important meal of the day. I absolutely must eat my breakfast or I cannot even think straight. Your body is hungry when you wake up because it has not had any food for several hours. If you skip your breakfast, chances are you will grab a candy bar or donut midmorning and throw your blood sugar for a loop. Studies have also shown that children who are not fed breakfast have a lower concentration level and do poorly on exams. If all else fails, they might eat a slice of whole grain bread or an apple with peanut butter. You can even buy boiled eggs in a bag to keep in your refrigerator for a quick nutritional breakfast.

Drink a little vino and preferably make it red wine. Indulge in red wine and reap the benefits of resveratrol, which helps keep plaque from sticking to the platelets of the heart and protects against inflammation. Resveratrol also protects your brain from that sticky nasty plaque seen in Alzheimer's patients.

Have a cup of Joe! I had a neighbor many years ago that used to have morning coffee with her young son. I thought it was so odd and I wondered if it was healthy for him to drink coffee; however, it certainly was healthier than soda and some fruit juices are nothing more than sugar water. His coffee was half milk and it was probably not a bad thing.

Life Extension recently reported a 13-year study done on coffee drinking habits and how it affected mortality. There were 400,000 men and women in the study conducted by National Institute of Health and AARP. The study monitored and documented participant's coffee consumption. The coffee drinkers had a higher survival rate. The more coffee they drank, the less likely they were to die. The test used both caffeinated and decaffeinated coffee and surprisingly it did not make a difference as to which type one drank. So, what was the key ingredient? Polyphenols in coffee are mega antioxidants that regulate many of the cell's processes. Coffee drinking drastically lowers the risk of developing age-related diseases such as cardiovascular disease, cognitive decline, cancer, diabetes, and inflammation. Forgo the soda and double lattes and drink a few cups of black coffee. Three cheers for our Joe!

Choose a dessert fit for a princess. Hale chocolate! This delectable food of the gods is loaded with flavonoids which, according to Cleveland Clinic doctors, helps protect against environmental pollutants. Flavonoids help repair damage done by free radicals. Chocolate was found to lower blood pressure and protect the heart in a way similar to red wine, which is to

Barbara Miller

keep that sticky plaque from forming and raising havoc with our artery walls.

Not all chocolate is created equal. Milk chocolate does not pack the same punch as dark chocolate. In fact, to get the most benefit from chocolate, it must have a high percentage of cocoa—at least 70 percent. Over-processing destroys the flavonoids and strips the cocoa of its health benefits. Dip a piece of extra dark chocolate into peanut butter and savor the delectable blended flavors. Most chocolate bars are laden with sugars, nuts, wax and unhealthy oils. It may taste heavenly but it will only land on your tummy. Try purchasing your dark chocolate at health food stores, Whole Foods or Trader Joe's. Check the ingredients first and enjoy!

A Mayo Clinic study found that people who actually adopted and faithfully continued to follow a Mediterranean type diet not only lost weight but lowered their cholesterol. When you begin eliminating unhealthy fat from your diet and add healthy fats like olive oil, you cannot help but lose weight. Keep nuts and fruit readily available. You may want to cut up fruits like watermelon, cantaloupe, papaya, and mangos to make them more enticing to eat whenever you or your kids need a snack.

We have a responsibility to our amazing body and it needs us to nourish and protect it by cutting down on meat and increasing fresh fruits and vegetables. Our bodies need dietary fiber and fruits and vegetables are the best ways to get it. Make nuts your snack and reach for an apple or orange for your treat—or a square of dark chocolate. Create your own Mediterranean-style blueprint for a healthy happy body.

- What are you doing to take charge of your life and your health?
- Are you giving up because you feel it is too late to get control of your body?
- Do you have a workout friend or partner to give you the support you need?
- Have you made health and fitness a priority in your life?

- Are you currently eating a healthy Mediterranean type diet?
- What does your future look like if you continue life as usual?

Start planning today for a healthy tomorrow and make the necessary changes to be the very best you possible. Make quality of life for you and those you love your number one priority. It is never too late to create change in your life.

*The secret of health for both mind and body is not to mourn for the past, worry about the future, or anticipate troubles, but to live in the present moment wisely and earnestly. "*Buddha

Chapter 8
DANCE OF SOLITUDE

*"Then because so many people were coming and going
that they did not even have a chance to eat, he said to
them,
"Come with me by yourselves to a quiet place and get
some rest." Mark 6:31*—Jesus of Nazareth, NIV
Bible

Muir Woods is without a doubt one of the most spiritual sanctuaries on earth. The canopy of giant Sequoias trees rises majestically toward the sun and spreads out enormous branches like a giant umbrella. They are the protectors of the flora and fauna that blanket the forest floor. Walking through Muir Woods was one of the most profound experiences in my entire life. No one spoke. You only dared whisper. There was a sacred hush and I felt as though I could hear the forest speak ever so softly. The soft trickling of a winding brook and moss-covered logs sprouting soft ferns created the essence of a holy shrine. It was only through this experience of awe and wonder that I understood John Muir and his lifelong odyssey to preserve our planet and all its richness and splendor. His spirit was truly present here and all one had to do to feel it was sit quietly and let your own spirit whisper back in this primordial sound of silence.

Barbara Miller

"A few minutes ago every tree was excited, bowing to the roaring storm, waving, swirling, and tossing their branches in glorious enthusiasm like worship. But though to the outer ear these trees are now silent, their songs never cease." John
Muir

While on a cruise with my husband David, we decided to take a side excursion in Dominica to a beautiful rainforest. We were there to go tubing down what were supposed to be *gentle rapids*. I started getting nervous when I was strapped into a heavy-duty life jacket but it was too late to turn back as I would have been left alone in the jungle. So off we hiked to get to the river and begin our mile *gentle ride* down. The river looked pretty calm as we slid on top of our inner tubes and lined up neatly in a row. Not too bad, I thought. Oh boy, it wasn't long before I began to feel the speed picking up; I tried to pretend I did not hear rushing rapids ahead. I struggled frantically to keep my inner tube balanced as many ahead of me were spinning out of control.

I watched in horror as three people flipped upside down then desperately attempted to grab their run-away inner tube. This was beginning to look more like Niagara Falls to me than gentle rapids! I saw a few people standing nearby and trying to reach others in trouble. I made it down without flipping and thought this must be the most difficult part of our ride. Wrong! I hit bubbling, churning rapids, and all I could think was 'I am going to die.' Over I went with a death grip on my inner tube. I was upside down, frantically attempting to avoid the rocks while choking and screaming at the same time. The next thing I knew, arms were grabbing me and pulling me to safety.

The last thing I wanted to do was climb back onto that inner tube, but one of our guides, whom by this point I hated, said, "It's okay, Miss. It is calm ahead and when we reach the end, there is a beautiful pool that is so calm it looks like glass." He could tell I was still shaken from my ordeal and didn't totally believe him. He said, "I will pull you and your tube the rest of the way until we get to the pool." Now that was a deal. He paddled us along while I relaxed and for the first time got to look around this magnificent forest. And sure enough, he had told the truth and he floated me to the middle of the most beautiful, breathtaking, calm pool I had ever seen. I took a few deep breaths and just simply allowed myself to be one with the nature around me. I left all my worrying, striving, thrashing and fear behind. I had left the churning rapids for the calmness of the sacred pool.

This is exactly what we need to do with life. Leave all the turmoil behind and step away to a quiet sacred space and quiet our minds, like the tranquil pool at the end of the rapids. Life can keep us churning and spinning until we feel like we are upside down and gasping for air. Retreating to a quiet place is what our soul needs to restore balance and peace once again.

Everyone needs beauty as well as bread, places to play in and pray in, where nature may heal and give strength to body and soul. John Muir

Retreat

Take time for yourself by stepping out of the fast-paced real world and into a quiet space. My dear friend Marilyn and I decided we needed a special "lady's day" for just the two of us. I suggested we try the Salt Cave as I had read about it in Awakenings Magazine and had always wanted to check it out. I called and made a reservation for us to spend an afternoon. We first met in a little Mediterranean restaurant for an early healthy lunch and then drove to the salt cave.

We started our mini retreat by each having a separate service. Marilyn had a Light Therapy treatment and I chose a Harmonious Bodywork massage. I had no clue what a Harmonious Bodywork massage meant, just that it sounded like something I needed; and it was amazing! The massage therapist used Himalayan crystal salt while massaging my body—it was wonderful. There was definitely an energy exchange as the healing hands of the therapist massaged my sore muscles. At one point, I actually felt an electrical shock in my left shoulder muscle as it was my most sensitive area. After this one-hour treatment, I felt so relaxed I just wanted to sleep.

The actual Salt Cave was where I met up again with Marilyn, who looked as blissful as I felt. We were told to remove our shoes and place a white nurse's cap on our heads to protect the pure salts in the cave. We were then instructed about what to expect during our quiet time. No talking was allowed as there might be others in the cave who wanted to meditate or sleep. We were directed to a lounge chair with a blanket and pillow and told that we would be in the cave for 45 minutes. We could lie on the lounge chair or a yoga mat on the floor and sleep or meditate whichever we chose.

Once our instructor left and my eyes adjusted to the darkened room, I looked around and studied this amazing space that really did look like a salt cave. There were large baskets holding big chunks of various shades of pink Himalayan crystal salt. There must have been thousands of shapes of salt throughout the cave, from the ceiling to the floor; even the walls were salt. I finally closed my eyes and remembered the instructions to breathe deeply to enjoy the healing benefits of the salt crystals. I began to tune into the soothing Zen music playing in the background and meditate on all that was peaceful and good. Even the sound of the motor from the dehumidifier used to keep the salt from absorbing moisture seemed far away.

The 45 minutes went by way too quickly; I wanted to stay longer but we each had another service scheduled. Our next treatment was a detox foot bath which was to remove toxins from the body. After we finished our appointment, we were shown around and instructed on the various uses of Himalayan Sea Salt. Our retreat had now come to an end and as we walked out into the bright Florida sunlight, we hugged goodbye and pledged not to wait so long for our next "*lady's day.*"

It is important to make time for friends because both your mind and body benefit from friends. For one thing, you are forced to use your memory, especially if you have mutual friends and experiences to talk about and remember. However, there is much more at stake and that is our sense of wellbeing and calmness. We are wired to socialize and share with friends and this exchange helps us feel connected and valuable.

My wonderful friend Karol recently gave me a surprise gift. It was a day at a local spa for the two of us. I was so excited and totally surprised. We decided not to have individual services as we wanted to just use the spa facility to visit and relax. We drove together to the spa and after checking in, we changed into our bathing suits and relaxed quietly in the meditation room. There were luxurious lounge beds with large fluffy towels, soft music and aromatherapy candles burning. After relaxing, we drank refreshing lemon water and then decided to get in the sauna and let our bodies do a little detoxing.

Next on our agenda was a walk on the beach as the spa was on beautiful Marco Island. We chatted quietly as we walked along, taking in the calm waters of the Gulf of Mexico, watching little Sandpipers darting in and out of the gentle surf. It was a perfect day at the beach as it was summer time in Florida. The beaches were mostly deserted, because the winter vacationers had gone home. The ocean sparkled in the sunlight as gulls soared and sang overhead.

After our walk, we opted for the Jacuzzi. It was so relaxing and we were the only two in the private courtyard. The day began to slip away as we basked in our time apart and it was a surprise when an attendant served us each a glass of champagne topped off with a large, chocolate-dipped strawberry. We lounged lazily, giggling and laughing at how much we loved feeling like princesses as our lunch was served in the quiet courtyard.

My daughter Alison and I have always been best friends and enjoy spending time together. A few years ago, when I was still living in Grand Rapids, Alison and I were lounging out on my deck and chatting. Alison expressed how she was going to be heading back to college in two weeks and wished we could have had time for a get-away weekend for just the two of us. I said "Where would you like to go?" "New York City," she responded quickly, because she had two vouchers for discount flights. I said, "Well, how about now?"

She literally flew off her chair and ran to the phone. I heard a conversation but could not hear what was being said. Suddenly she screamed, "Mother, pack your suitcase. I am taking the dogs to the kennel; we leave in one hour!" I stood up, dazed, thinking how did I get myself into this situation? "Hurry," she ordered, as she ran out the door with my two dogs.

At this point, all I did was follow orders. I threw on my white pantsuit and grabbed a few things for a carry-on bag and called it done. I drove us to the airport, which fortunately was only 10 minutes away. I pulled up to our airline gate and dropped her off to check us in and you guessed it, it was before 9/11. I flew into the terminal and saw her flailing her arms at me to hurry up. We both ran to catch our flight.

Once we settled down and caught our breath, we looked at each other and burst out laughing. We were both wearing white pantsuits! A man leaned over and said, "Are you girls flight attendants?" "No," I said, "we are twins." The second we were airborne, we ordered wine, actually mine could have been stronger, and then it hit me. We had no hotel reservations! I turned to Alison and said, "What are we going to do and where are we going to stay?" Her favorite words, "Oh no problem, Mother, we will find a room." I envisioned us sleeping in Central Park.

As soon as we arrived in New York City, we got on the phone with hotels. I just happened to remember a hotel I had stayed at during a skincare convention and I was so relieved that they had a room; however, the hotel clerk informed me that there were two large conventions in New York City that weekend and they could only take us for one night. We would have to be out of our room by 11:00 am.

Alison knew of a hotel in Times Square she had stayed at with a friend a couple of years ago and sure enough they had a room for our second night. It was not exactly the greatest hotel but it was not Central Park, and all we needed was a place to sleep.

The first day started by wandering around New York, just window shopping. We took a cab to Greenwich Village and had lunch in a quaint vintage restaurant. We spent about two hours just laughing and people watching and then roamed the streets looking through various shops. We finely took a cab to Soho and checked out the various funky boutiques. Then we headed back to our hotel to change for dinner in Little Italy, but not before working our way through China Town and being accosted by fake purse and watch hawkers.

What fun we had that weekend, complete with afternoon tea at the Russian Tea House. It was rather wild and crazy and definitely outrageous, but a very special time with just the two of us taking time to come together and enjoy each other and live in the moment. We still reminisce about that spontaneous weekend and laugh at the split-second decision that turned out to be so rewarding.

I will always cherish those times shared with my dearest friends and remember to give thanks that I am so blessed. Take time out with your special friend, even if it is meeting at

Starbuck's for coffee; as long as you make it special and just for the two of you. Don't be afraid to leap fearlessly and dare to embrace all that life has to offer.

Meditation

You do not have to take a trip in order to step away from all the noise and turmoil of life, sometimes a few minutes of silent meditation is just what we need. Practicing *mindfulness meditation* is a great way to bring calmness and centeredness to the churning rapids of our lives. What is mindfulness meditation? It is an exercise of focusing on the present moment and not allowing outside thoughts to creep in, like 'What is for dinner tonight?' Meditation is also about proper breathing. That is why guided meditation encourages concentration on your breath, which helps keep your mind from wandering.

While meditating, try stepping away from yourself like a silent observer and just concentrate on your breathing—slowly in—slowly out. Sense the quiet spaces. Do you like yourself in these quiet spaces? Are you okay with yourself for company? Get alone with you—go to a quiet place and get some rest. You may have had a friend or family member try and counsel you at some stage of your life. Their advice might be to try and get your mind off your problems by doing something constructive and stop focusing on everything that is wrong in your life or health. It is good advice and if you really could step away from yourself and look back, what might you see? Often, we are too close to the problem and that is all we can see. Expand your space outward and unwrap your cellophane. As acceptance of

yourself and your life expands to create more space for life—
the focus is turned outward instead of being self-absorbed.

Many doctors are now encouraging stressed out patients to
meditate. It restores balance from anxiety or depression. It helps
bring calmness to those with chronic heart conditions and
attention deficit disorder. If it is too difficult to focus on your
breathing then try citing your own personal mantra, something
like, *"I feel calm and peaceful as I breathe in and breathe out."*
Meditation is all about calming the mind and clearing away the
fog.

I decided I wanted to learn Buddhist Meditation from a
trained leader. I found a local Buddhist temple and with more
than a little apprehension I joined a group of about twenty
people. As I walked in the room, I noticed people taking off their
shoes and placing them in tiny cubicles. The leader welcomed
me and gave a few instructions, while others offered to walk in
with me. I was grateful and felt really self-conscious. Everyone
gave a slight bow to a Buddha statue, as a sign of respect I was
told. Several sat around on chairs and others sat in the traditional
Buddha posture on pillows on the floor.

The atmosphere was entirely relaxed. I did not see anyone
rushing in and frantically searching for a seat. There was only a
sense of calmness. I felt incredibly awkward as I explained to
the woman sitting next to me that I had an allergy cough and the
incense in the room might trigger my cough. She looked at me
calmly and said, "Everybody coughs at times, Barbara."
"Okay," I mumbled as I tried to breathe deeply and relax. The
leader began by instructing everyone to find their breath and

listen to it. "Breathe in slowly and fill up, then slowly and effortlessly breathe out. Breathe in and out with eyes closed."

After fifteen minutes, we were instructed to stand and walk in a circle following the person in front of us. I stood up and turned around the wrong way and startled myself as I was facing, not following. I was embarrassed upon hearing a few chuckles as I spun around and headed in the right direction. After fifteen minutes of walking, we sat down again and were brought back to our breathing.

I finally relaxed and became less aware of others in the room. As I sat with my eyes closed and focused on my breathing; suddenly, without warning, a large eye appeared in the middle of my forehead. It was blue just like mine and it appeared to be looking right into me! My eyes popped open and my deep breathing came to an abrupt halt. I looked around and everyone else still had their eyes closed. I wanted to shout, what was that? I had heard of the *third eye* before but I certainly had never seen it. What was its purpose and why was it looking back at me? It shook me up so much that I just could not sit there any longer. The session was two hours and as far as I was concerned, it was an hour too long. I slid out of my chair, dropped my love offering in the bowl and promptly got out of there.

I went straight home and looked up the *third eye* on my computer. The *third eye* is considered the inner gate to higher consciousness. It is also called the sixth sense and some believe that it is controlled by the pineal gland. Evidently, I had been able to relax enough that I opened up to my higher consciousness. The *third eye* is our intuition, and meditation hones your intuitive skills, allowing you to access your inner feelings. Intuition means *to see within* and the ability to know something without thinking or conscious awareness. Meeting someone for the first time and having a "gut feeling" about their intention is an example of intuition.

Meditation is a great way to hone your intuitive skills because it quiets the mind and wakes up your intuition. Some have a more developed intuitive power than others. Many have expressed finding answers to issues in their lives through mindfulness meditation. I have found that over-focusing on a question or problem can stifle intuition. However, relaxing my mind through meditation seems to free my intuition to provide the answers I am looking for. Meditation is the perfect way to slip away to a quiet place and relax.

The Diagnostic Clinic in London studied the effects of meditation physiologically. The study was headed by medical director, Doctor Rajendra Sharma. Dr. Sharma says, *"People who meditate automatically counteract stress chemicals and so reduce stress-related illnesses such as stomach ulcers and recurrent flu and colds."* He goes on to explain how those who meditate have less illness and faster healing compared to the non-meditators. Author of *The Charge*, Brendon Burchard, says, *"Meditate. Neuroscience has proven that meditation is powerful not only in reducing stress levels, but also in growing neurons and activating our capacities for more creativity, empathy, and achievement."* Wow, all the more reasons to meditate!

Meditation does not have to be done in a seated position, although this is the traditional method. However, you can get similar benefits by walking in a quiet place and staying focused on your breathing. Calming the mind and finding your center through meditation produces deep relaxation which increases blood flow and lowers blood pressure.

The basics of meditation are the same, with the emphasis always on your breathing. Breathe into your belly and feel it expand and then slowly exhale until your belly begins to tighten, and repeat. Make certain you find a time and place where you will not be interrupted. Also, your clothing should not be too tight as you want nothing to restrict your breathing or be distracting. I like to sit in a chair and mentally go through a relaxing routine of focusing on my body and then shifting to my breathing. Staying in the moment helps reduce anxiety.

Perhaps you have fears that continuously come to mind and block your efforts to relax. You may want to try this exercise—call all of your fears to attention—then take them one by one. Don't let them all jump out at once and attempt to compete for credit as your "biggest fear." Next, call forth fear number one and ask it some frank questions—what do you want and why are you tormenting me? Why should I fear you? It may try and fool you by appearing larger so don't be afraid to call its bluff. Tell your fear that you are only interested in the truth. Breathe deeply and slowly as you calmly call forth each fear or worry. Now mentally step outside yourself and allow your fear to sit in your chair. Look at it—study it and calmly watch it disappear. It is only able to exist in your imagination, and when you refuse to give it life—it leaves!

Maybe acknowledging your fear, will help shed some light on an idea or a plan to overcome this particular fear or perhaps it will help you see how you have given it too much life and helped it grow into a full-blown monster. Most fear lives only in our imagination and calling its bluff by not giving any more sacred space to it, will send it packing. The important thing is to stop wrestling with your fear and replace it with peace.

There are several types of CDs available if you prefer to meditate with soft music in the background. There are also many free guided meditations on the internet. Discover what works best for you. Meditation is the perfect way to *quiet your mind* and get some rest.

There are times in my life when I imagine myself standing on the edge of the earth—just like the dancer on the cover of this book. I bow my head and step into the Universe. Sometimes I feel alone and frightened so I walk forward and climb up into the Creator's lap and just stay there for a while, feeling safe and protected like a small child. However, at other times, I am there for a petition and wearing my princess crown and a long glittering gown. I bow my head as angels shake their wings and shower me with sparkling jewels. They create a jewel-covered pathway for me to walk and they hover above as I state my request. I can visit this sacred place just by closing my eyes and envisioning it. You can also create your own special sacred place where you can feel safe and get away from the stresses of life.

- What is your favorite way or place to step apart and get some rest?
- Do you take time for yourself to reflect and mediate?
- Are you staying connected to friends and family members?
- What steps could you take to reconnect with those you love?

- Do you need to slow down and get off the speeding treadmill?

Eileen Fisher in a letter to her younger self

"Stillness is the ground of being from which all else emerges. It is within and behind every breath, every thought, every action. It is my starting point, my resting place, the home base to which I can return again and again. In stillness I notice how time and space disappear. All there is, is the present moment and my willingness to listen and to allow the stillness to speak"

Chapter 9
DANCE OF LOVE

"Absence diminishes small loves and increases great ones, as the wind blows out the candle and fans the bonfire." Francois Duc de La Rochefoucauld

Oh love, sweet Eros, God of love, son of Aphrodite. How we all long for Prince Charming to gallop into our lives and fight to save the beautiful princess and slay the dragon. He scoops us up into his lap as we gallop off to his castle to be wed and live happily ever after.

Helen Fisher, author of *Why We Love*, relates love to the body's need to sleep and eat. Fisher based her findings on the brain scans of those who had just fallen in love. The saying "loves knows no bounds" apparently is true. Romantic love has spurred such love tragedies as Romeo and Juliet and Mark Anthony and Cleopatra, and in more modern days, King Edward III of England and Wallace Simpson, a wealthy American socialite. Wallace Simpson had been divorced twice and was considered an unsuitable match for the king. However, nothing could deter the king from marrying Wallace. He submitted his abdication and resigned as monarch. The following is an excerpt from his infamous speech. *"But you must believe me when I tell you that I have found it impossible to carry the heavy burden of responsibility and to discharge my duties as King as I would wish to do without the help and support of the woman I love."*

Edward and Wallace had been married for 35 years when Edward died. Wallace was the true love of his life. To fall in love is to abandon all reason to anything except to gaze into the eyes of the beloved.

The Song of Solomon from the Bible tells a beautiful graphic story of passion, lust, and eroticism. However, King Solomon met his match when he attempted to seduce the Shulamite woman, whom many believe to have been the Queen of Sheba. Some have suggested that she was young, immature and unsure of herself, and perhaps afraid she would not please Solomon. I say she was mature and wise beyond her years. Her hesitation was clever and it sparked Solomon's interest even more. By the time she finally consented, Solomon was completely enraptured with her.

There really is power in that kiss as Cher's famous song tells us: "If you want to know if he loves you so, it's in his kiss." *Prevention* magazine published an article in their August issue, 2011, "Power of a Kiss." I was shocked to learn that a man's salvia contains testosterone and when kissing his love interest, dopamine is sent surging through—not just him—but her! Dopamine stimulates the brain just the same as if you had just used cocaine! So, if you want to keep the fire flaming, plant a juicy kiss on your beloved.

Thus, the saying, "madly in love" may explain why some have literally died for their love. I know men who have driven hundreds of miles and even hitchhiked all night just to spend one day with their love. Love actually alters our body chemistry—making us giddy and downright sickening. We write poems, songs, and letters professing our undying love. Humans love with reckless abandonment. The question is why?

According to an article in the January, 2008 issue of *Time* magazine, it's all about the smell. The love interest must smell of the right pheromones. You all know the old song, First Comes Love, Then Comes Marriage: however, the real song should be "First Comes Scent, Then Comes Testosterone." Your scent is magical. It tells the male which females would be compatible to conceive, and helps them zero in and connect with the one they want. Once he is in the position to plant his juicy testosterone-laden kiss, it can seal the deal. He is smitten! If he tastes and smells right—it equals *love gone mad*! This might explain why the frumpy unattractive competition walks off with the handsome hunk.

Dopamine is not the only drug involved at this point. Enter oxytocin—the bonding substance. This is when we need to be careful and step back to breathe. With all the chemicals racing through the body and brain, we can make mistakes. He may have seemed like "*the one*" last night, especially mixed with a little wine and great kissing, but he didn't call the next day like he promised.

Remember oxytocin, the bonding chemical? Women are far more susceptible to bonding than men. This is why jumping into bed with him on a first date is so dangerous. You may think he feels more for you than he actually does. You think it was love—he thinks he got laid! This age-old scenario has happened to many women who have shared with me how confused they were over a man they felt bonded or connected to, only to never hear from him again. He needed more time and excitement in his pursuit and a chance to play the *wooing role*. He wants to conquer and strut his stuff. Don't just hand over the prize— make him win it!

Eros love is passion, lust and longing with sensual desire for the lover. Plato says that Eros, the god of Love, can help the soul to remember beauty in its pure form. We get our English word 'erotic' from the Greek word 'Eros.' Eros love envelopes passion and chemistry between two lovers, although it is possible that one might be non-responsive to the sexual passionate desire of another. However, a relationship that is totally based on pure lust and sensual desire usually ends as quickly as it began. If it was pure lust and a feel-good experience with no solid foundation to build on, when it no longer excites and the sensual pleasure ceases, it is bye, bye love.

Many are in love with love and without their love fix they feel lost and incomplete. However, living in a state of unconditional love will fill that gap and free you to love yourself and not need outside love to complete you—you are already complete. When we learn to love ourselves, it frees us to love others unconditionally. Instead of trying to draw love to you, let it flow from you and create a never-ending circle of love.

> *There is more to sex appeal than just measurements. I don't need a bedroom to prove my womanliness. I can convey just as much sex appeal, picking apples off a tree or standing in the rain.* Audrey Hepburn, actress

The need to love is as fundamental as the need to breathe. Love will melt a lover's heart and will also break it. Helen Fisher, an anthropologist who researches why we love, likens romantic love to the rush of cocaine and says, "Romantic love is a powerful and primordial mating drive that evolved to find and keep life's most precious gift—an appropriate mating partner."

Barbara's Story

Meeting David only six weeks after moving to Naples, Florida was totally unexpected. He was so handsome and intelligent with a great sense of humor and I was drawn to him from the first time our eyes locked. I was thrilled to learn that he was single and unattached. We began a courtship that steadily blossomed into deep love for one another. We were so compatible; he was like a male version of me. I had never been so happy.

David came by one evening and said he had something to discuss with me. I had absolutely no idea what he would say. We had been dating a few months at this point. He explained that prior to meeting me; he had planned a boat trip up the coast from Florida all the way to Maine. Since his boat, Mon Ami, was a trawler and only went ten knots, the trip would take three months. He invited me to go but I declined as I had just started my new job. David said he would not go if I asked him not to because he did not want to lose me. He assured me he would fly back to Naples after a month and spend a week and would fly me up once he got to Maine.

I sat there stunned as this was totally unexpected. I thought for a moment before I responded. I said, "I think you should definitely go on your trip because clearly it is something you truly want to do, and I will not stand in your way." He once again reiterated saying, "I won't go if you say no." I insisted that he should go on his trip and all the while my heart nearly broke.

David flew back to Naples as he had promised and stayed for a week. That first month was long one, but he called every day and shared his adventure. I have never felt lonelier in my entire life. I was waking up from a sound sleep in the middle of the night crying.

I really had no idea just how much I would miss him and it actually felt painful.

Finally, it was time for me to fly up to Maine. I could tell he was more than excited to see me and he had planned to ensure that I would have an enjoyable time. It was so romantic and we could not get enough of each other. We had lobster picnics in Maine and sat on the boat in harbors, watching the curious wise-looking old seals swimming by staring up at us. The craggy shore with lobster traps as far as the eye could see had an ambiance all its own. I hated to have to go home and David clearly did not want me to leave.

Once I returned to Naples, David started calling more frequently and romantically expressing how much he missed me. He even suggested that maybe this trip was not such a great idea. Finally, after I had been home for a week, he called to say he was coming home two weeks early as he could not bear to be away from me. He nearly burned up the engines on Mon Ami trying to get home to me. Yes!

Once David returned home, he pledged to me that he was never going to leave my side again, and he never has. The bottom line is that I fully believe being apart for that period of time would either fan our flame or burn it out. Had I begged him not to go, I would have been the loser. By letting him follow his dream I got back many times more than I gave up—a proposal!

We have been together for ten years and happily married for seven years. I hated having him gone from me for so long, but the payback has been amazing!

Mike Dooley, author of *Infinite Possibilities, The Art of Living Your Dreams*, says, "*If your desire or dream is to win over someone's heart as a means to achieving your own happiness, somehow you've come to believe that your happiness depends on the approval or the company of another, which simply isn't true.*" We have been taught from the time we were little girls that one day we would meet our perfect match and fall madly in love. We would marry and have children and live in married bliss. That old story is actually a really sick joke to play on unsuspecting little girls. If this story were true, we would not have nearly half of all marriages fail.

We definitely need a whole new approach to our views on love and marriage. I think a textbook written just for girls in junior high school is in order, along with classes that go on throughout high school instructing girls as to what marriage and babies really means. Men need their own textbook to cover their unrealistic expectations on the definition of marriage. We are expected to make a commitment that lasts for most of our adult life and in reality, not have a clue as to what we are getting ourselves into or what to expect. Little girls grow up and play house and many end up prisoners of their own reality. Playing house for keeps is not fun and games, it is hard work!

Remember the wonderful movie, The King and I, with Yul Brynner and Deborah Kerr? It was based on the true story of Mongkut, the King of Siam and Anna Leonowens, who travelled from England to be the live-in governess to the King's royal children. The King and Anna fell in love but the religious and cultural differences were so drastically incompatible that Anna finally left and returned to England.

My favorite part of the movie was when the King wanted to learn to dance. Anna at first refused, but the King insisted and she finally acquiesced to his wishes and taught him how to dance. I held my breath during that entire scene, it was so romantic. However, would this have been a realistic union? No, probably not. Anna knew she would be part of a harem and she was a widow with a young son. She could have lived in the lap of luxury but she courageously defended her beliefs and refused to compromise her life and that of her son. Anna and the King stayed in touch with each other until his death.

- Are you still waiting for Prince Charming to ride in scoop you up and make your life complete?
- Do you have realistic views on how to attract the man of your dreams?
- How would you define the qualities of your ideal man?

Barbara Miller

- Are you anticipating your ideal man to provide happiness?
- Have you clearly defined your life purpose?
- Is your current behavior leading you closer to that purpose?

If the habits you have been following to find the man of your dreams are not working for you and you are still lonely and unhappy, maybe it is time to consider a new approach. Very often, creating a new focus will take the pressure off and allow you to relax and give space to nurture your own soul. We all want someone to love; however, being loved in return is the most important ingredient. Love often comes softly and if you are striving frantically to find a man, you will miss the quiet one standing on the sidelines admiring you.

> *"Pain is a great motivator that breaks down the walls that keep old behaviors intact. Pain guides us toward thoughts and ideas that we might otherwise push away, and it forces us to seek answers from places we have never looked before."*
> Debbie Ford

Chapter 10
DANCING WITH THE UNIVERSE

"Everything has rhythm, everything dances."
Maya Angelou

It is impossible to avoid adversity and change in our life. Just as seasons come and go in order to bring forth new growth, so it is with each individual life. The dormant times do not always feel so good and we often fail to recognize that we must be still and make space for our own soul's renewal. Just as the spring gives birth to beautiful blossoms that burst into color, it is the final stage that bears the fruit that nourishes our body.

Take time to feed your soul and reflect in the quiet times what great happiness and gifts the Universe has already bestowed on you. Lighten up—it's a great feeling! Clean out, close out, weed out, and expand your space. Live life more fully and outrageously! Love passionately and give space to welcome what is yet to come. Give up on always having to be right. Receive help when you need it, give praise, and graciously accept it!

You do have a choice in how far you let your feelings go and what you decide to focus on. We are not always going to feel good about our life and that is okay. Things are not always going to run smoothly; there will be rocky roads, detours and dead-end streets but we do not have to abandon ship to get control of our life. Maybe we simply need to pause, and evaluate the situation. If you are at an impasse, maybe you need to make some life-changing choices. Remember the old poem we learned in school as kids? *Stop, look, and listen before you cross the street, use your eyes, use your ears, and then you use your feet.* It is pretty simple but sound advice even today.

Quit living your life as a victim, constantly complaining about everything that is wrong. Maybe it is time to *stop* blaming others, own up to the truth, and take responsibility for your own life story. It is not always somebody else's fault. If you spend your life continually moaning and groaning about your circumstances, you will miss out living a joyful meaningful life. Be still and *listen* for a change. Are you ready to take responsibility and acknowledge your bad behavior or mistakes, or are you still accusing and blaming everyone else for making your life miserable?

You might have had a frightening childhood like me, and if you did, I am truly sorry you had to go through that kind of trauma. However, we cannot go back and rewrite our past to a Leave It to Beaver, fantasy childhood. It is over and it is up to you to close that chapter. I did not have any control over my childhood, but now I do have control of my life. It is time to write your own chapter starting with—NOW! Not yesterday— not tomorrow—but NOW. Try stepping back and *looking* at yourself as others might see you. Take inventory and ask: *Is this what I really want to be doing? Is this what I want my legacy to be?* If not, it is time for a new dance.

Remember my story earlier about my friend Marilyn zip-lining through the jungle? Well, I could hardly wait to try zip-lining and I finally got my chance. While on a trip to Virgin Gorda in the British Virgin Islands, we found a ziplining excursion. We got on a tour bus that took a group out to the jungle. I was so excited and at the same time scared to death! When they strapped me into the harness and fitted me with a hard hat and thick gloves, I started having flashbacks of my tubing excursion. Oh boy! I then noticed this elderly couple and I thought 'What in the world are they thinking?' We walked to our first station and climbed a few steps and one by one we were hooked up to the line and instructed as they pushed us off for our first adventure.

I thought 'So far so good' and I actually might live through this madness. However, as we got to our next stations, the steps were higher and took far more effort to get to the top of the trees. We started noticing the elderly couple was struggling to climb to the top. They kept stopping to catch their breath and others were assisting them. I thought 'oh my goodness, they should not be out here; it is far too dangerous for people their age.' However, there was no way back through the jungle except the zip lines that would now carry us back at over 50 feet up and 50 miles per hour! What was I thinking!

I had noticed earlier that each of the trees where we zip-lined to, had padding on them. All I was thinking at that point was 'Thank God' because I might just go slamming into that tree. I flew in at the speed of light while the guides were yelling, "Slow down!" I crashed into both of them and then hit the tree. Fortunately, they broke my speed enough that I was okay. David came crashing in right behind me and, much to our horror, we both stood with mouths gapping open as the older woman came screaming in! She flew right through the guards and hit the tree, face first. As she stood there hugging the tree, we totally expected to watch her slither down unconscious, but no way! She stepped back shook her head, turned around threw her arms up and yelled, "I did it!" Along came her husband with the same exact scenario, "I did it!" Everyone cheered and screamed, "Yeah!"

I was ashamed of myself for judging them and their ability and desire for adventure. Maybe it was also on their *bucket list*— I applaud them and their courage. That zip-lining experience was a life lesson for me in conquering fear and following my dream. Whatever you have on your bucket list, no matter how old you are—do it! You are enough—imperfections and all. Don't be afraid to be vulnerable or you may never realize your dreams. It is normal to be afraid of being exposed, but if we compromise our deepest desires out of fear of criticism, then we may lose out on an amazing future.

> *"You may not control all the events that happen to you, but you can decide not to be reduced by them."* Maya Angelou

Mike Dooley, author of *Infinite Possibilities, the Art of Living Your Dreams*, says, *"Whatever your level of understanding, it will not change the fact that you already create the life you lead from the thoughts you think; this truth cannot be escaped."* The answers to your life are held within you. They are just waiting to unfold and reveal themselves. Do the following exercise and see what you might discover that perhaps has been lying dormant in your life. Start by asking yourself the following questions. Just start writing. Don't think too long on the answers—just write! Resist putting up any road blocks which will stall your creative energy. Remember my Fire Walk? Yes I can, yes I can, yes YOU can! You have all heard the song, "Oh wild thing, what makes your heart sing?"

- Who am I? Just start writing.
- What makes me happy?
- What makes me sad?
- What makes me excited?
- What challenges me?
- When do I most feel fulfilled?
- What's on my bucket list?

Now put your paper aside and come back to it later. Many are surprised at what they wrote. There are clues you have written for the life you want. Start today with just one step to move you closer to your heart's desire.

You reflect the beauty of creation—a one of a kind masterpiece with immense value. You are a signed original work of art crafted by the hand of the Master Creator of the Universe. The Creator has blessed you with intelligence and the power to choose your own life path. What story is painted on your own personal canvas?

Finding your own center and creating a rhythm and flow that frees you to manifest the life you truly want and so richly deserve can be accomplished by mastering the art of developing the 10 steps outlined for you in this book. You will gain clarity for your goals and desires for your life because life will manifest your dance exactly as you choreographed it.

Barbara Miller

"Nobody cares if you can't dance well. Just get up and dance.
Great dancers are not great because of their technique;
they are great because of their passion.

Martha Graham

Don't be afraid to let go of things that no longer serve you well. Determine to shake off old restricting habits and outmoded beliefs and leap fearlessly into your new life. Change can be ever so painful, yet accepting change might just be the catalyst that opens up new life experiences more exciting than you ever dreamed. When my former husband left me for a younger woman, I thought my life was over and that I would never find happiness again. I tried desperately to hang on to my past life. However, it was not until I finally let go and accepted and released that part of my life, that I was able to heal and focus on the present. When you continue to seek joy and completeness through some future event, you rob yourself of all that is possible at this moment!

Will you fill your space with pain or light? Constantly living in the past gives life to the pain you experienced. Continuing in this vein will keep you paralyzed, stuck and fearful. Stop allowing yourself to be ruled by your school of pain. It has taught you well but it was a school of deception. You are not your pain. The Power of Now lays out a profound blueprint for finally understanding and expanding into Source. You are the key and you dictate to life the dance you want it to perform.

And each day as you stand before the Universe in its entire splendor on the edge of consciousness, I'll be there— cheering you on, challenging your motives and praising your choices as you trust the Universe to bring all your desires and dreams to fruition. I'll be shouting, "Yes you can! Bravo, Princesses of the Universe—Bravo!" Allow yourself to live life fearlessly with outrageous abandonment!

"Tune into the presence of miracles, and in an instant, life can be transformed into a dazzling experience, more wondrous and exciting than we could even imagine."

Deepak Chopra

If you would like further information about Barbara, please visit the Barbara & Company website at:

www.barbaraandcompany.com

www.ketoforlifeblog.com

You will find information on the website about Barbara's weight loss program based on her book *Keto for Life, 28 Day Fat-Fueled Approach to Weight Loss.*

Dancing in Rhythm with the Universe is available at:

www.barbaraandcompany.com

www.amazon.com

www.barnesandnoble.com

About the Author

Barbara Miller, author, motivational speaker, and certified Master Life Coach, is the founder of Barbara & Company International, Inc. Barbara inspires women through her books, coaching, lectures, and blog to access their power, inner beauty and spirit, to take charge and create the life they truly want to lead. Through her work, the author has met dozens of women who struggle to choreograph the life they want to dance. Barbara shares her own challenges through change and loss, and then provides examples and direction to encourage the reader to step out of conflict and fear and open up to the miracles of the Universe! Learn to walk right through inner fears and fall into perfect alignment, *Dancing in Rhythm with the Universe.*

Connect with Barbara on Facebook:

www.facebook. com/barbaramillerauthor

Follow Barbara on Twitter:

www.twitter.com/barbarasmiller

CITED WORKS

Chapter One

The Power of Now: A Guide to Spiritual Enlightenment by Eckhart Tolle, New World Library, 2004

The Art of Happiness, 10th Anniversary Addition, A Handbook for *Living* by His Holiness The Dali Lama and Howard C. Cutler, Riverhead Books, 2009

Chapter Seven

Calming Your Anxious Mind: How Mindfulness and Compassion Can Free You From Anxiety, Fear and Panic by Jeffery Brantley, M. D., Raincoast Books, 2007

The 9 Step to Keep the Doctor Away: Simple Actions to Shift Your Body and Mind to Optimum Health for Greater Longevity by Dr. Rashid A. Buttar, GMEC Publishing, 2010

Chapter Eight

The Charge: Activating the 10 Human Drives That Make You Feel Alive by Brendon Burchard, Free Press, 2012 by Helen Fisher, St. Martin's Griffin, 2004

Infinite Possibilities: The Art of Living Your Dreams by Mike Dooley, Atria Books, 2009

Chapter Nine

Why We Love: The Nature and Chemistry of Romantic Love by Helen Fisher

Infinite Possibilities: The Art of Living Your Dreams by Mike Dooley

SUGGESTED READING

Sexy Forever: How to Fight Fat After Forty by Suzanne Somers, Crown Archetype, 2010

Think: Straight Talk for Women to Stay Smart in a Dumbed-Down World by Lisa Bloom, Vanguard Press, 2011

Heart of the Matter: How to Find Love—How to Make it Work by Linda Austin, M.D., Atria Books, 2003

The Courage to be Yourself: A Woman's Guide to Emotional Strength and Self-Esteem by Sue Patton Thoele, Conari Press, 2001

The Seat of the Soul by Larry Zukav, Fireside, 1990

Self Matters: Creating Your Life from the Inside Out by Phillip C. McGraw, Ph.D., Free Press, 2003

You Can Heal Your Life by Louise L. Hay, Hay House,1987

He's Just Not That Into You: The No-Excuse Truth to Understanding Guys by Greg Behrendt and Liz Tuccillo, Simon Schuster, Inc., 2006

Barbara Miller

Choose Them Wisely: Thoughts Become Things by Mike Dooley, Atria Books, 2009

Excuses Be Gone!: How to Change Lifelong, Self-Defeating Thinking Habits by Dr. Wayne W. Dyer, Hay House 2009

www.ingramcontent.com/pod-product-compliance
Lightning Source LLC
Chambersburg PA
CBHW030012290326
41934CB00005B/311